MEETING THE CHALLENGE

GOAL

Ranger Rick's Nature-Scope *is a creative education series dedicated to inspiring in children an understanding and appreciation of the natural world while developing the skills they will need to make responsible decisions about the environment.*

I t has been almost a decade since the publication of the first *Endangered Species: Wild and Rare* in the **Ranger Rick's NatureScope** series. Since that time, we have had both encouraging and discouraging news about the environment. Our awareness has been heightened and much has been done, but there is still much to do.

One of the best ways to ensure sustained concern for our planet and the creatures who inhabit it is to educate our children. This new edition of *Endangered Species: Wild and Rare* brings to the classroom the original material which has survived the test of time, along with new essays by and about people working in the field today, people who are still learning about how our environment works and who are taking action to preserve it. Here also is the sense of wonder they feel as they work in the natural world. This new edition also includes an updated bibliography for further study and enrichment.

The effort to save wildlife and habitat will span many generations. Like all lifelong commitments, there is no better time to begin than when we are young.

National Wildlife Federation

ENDANGERED SPECIES
WILD AND RARE

Other Titles in *Ranger Rick's NatureScope*

Ranger Rick's NatureScope

ENDANGERED SPECIES
WILD AND RARE

National Wildlife Federation

LEARNING TRIANGLE PRESS

*Connecting
kids, parents, and teachers
through learning*

An imprint of McGraw-Hill

New York San Francisco Washington, D.C. Auckland Bogotá Caracas
Lisbon London Madrid Mexico City Milan Montreal New Delhi
San Juan Singapore Sydney Tokyo Toronto

Library of Congress Cataloging-in-Publication Data applied for

McGraw-Hill

A Division of The McGraw·Hill Companies

NATIONAL WILDLIFE FEDERATION®

1 2 3 4 5 6 7 8 9 JDL/JDL 9 0 2 1 0 9 8 7

ISBN 0-07-046508-8

NatureScope® was originally conceived by National Wildlife Federation's School Programs Editorial Staff, under the direction of Judy Braus, Editor. Special thanks to all of the Editorial Staff, Scientific, Educational Consultants and Contributors who brought this series of eighteen publications to life.

NATIONAL WILDLIFE FEDERATION EDITORIAL STAFF
Creative Services Manager: Sharon Schiliro
Editor, Ranger Rick® magazine: Gerry Bishop
Director Classroom–related Programs: Margaret Tunstall
Contributors: Carol Boggis, Rhonda Lucas Donald, Sharon Levy, Susan Makurat–Bond

McGRAW-HILL EDP STAFF
Acquisitions Editor: Judith Terrill-Breuer
Editorial Supervisor: Patricia V. Amoroso
Production Supervisor: Claire Stanley
Designer: Jaclyn J. Boone
Cover Design: David Saylor

McGraw-Hill books are available at special quantity discounts to use as premiums and sales promotions, or for use in corporate training programs. For more information, please write to the Director of Special Sales, McGraw-Hill, 11 West 19th Street, New York, NY 10011. Or contact your local bookstore.

Printed and bound by the John D. Lucas Printing Company.
This book is printed on recycled and acid–free paper.

TM and ® designate trademarks of National Wildlife Federation and are used, under license, by The McGraw-Hill Companies, Inc.

RRNS

Endangered Species
Wild and Rare

TABLE OF CONTENTS

A Close-Up Look At Endangered Species: Wild And Rare

L ooking at the Table of Contents, you can see we've divided *Endangered Species: Wild and Rare* into four chapters (each of which deals with a broad endangered species theme), a craft section, and an appendix. Each of the four chapters includes *background information* that explains concepts and vocabulary, *activities* that relate to the chapter theme, and *Copycat Pages* that reinforce many of the concepts introduced in the activities.

You can choose single activity ideas or teach each chapter as a unit. Either way, each activity stands by itself and includes teaching objectives, a list of materials needed, suggested age groups, subjects covered, and a step-by-step explanation of how to do the activity. (The objectives, materials, age groups, and subjects are highlighted in the left-hand margin for easy reference.)

AGE GROUPS

The suggested age groups are:
- Primary (grades K-2)
- Intermediate (grades 3-5)
- Advanced (grades 6-7)

Each chapter usually begins with primary activities and ends with intermediate or advanced activities. But don't feel bound by the grade levels we suggest. Resourceful teachers, naturalists, parents, and club leaders can adapt most of these activities to fit their particular age group and needs.

OUTDOOR ACTIVITIES

We've included several outdoor activities in this issue. These are coded in the chapters in which they appear with this symbol:

COPYCAT PAGES

The *Copycat Pages* supplement the activities and include ready-to-copy games, puzzles, coloring pages, and/or worksheets. Look at the bottom of each Copycat Page for the name and page number of the activity that it goes with. *Answers to all Copycat Pages are in the texts of the activities.*

WHAT'S AT THE END

The fifth section, *Crafty Corner,* will give you some art and craft ideas that complement many of the activities in the first four chapters. And the last section, the *Appendix,* is loaded with reference suggestions that include books, films, and posters. The *Appendix* also has an endangered species glossary, suggestions for where to get more endangered species information, and a summary of the laws that protect threatened and endangered species.

THE BIG PICTURE

dodo

Scientists have identified and cataloged more than one and one-half million of the species that exist on Earth today. By some recent estimates, at least 20 times that many species inhabit the planet. But we're losing many of these plant and animal species even before they are discovered. And each year, more and more of the species we *do* know about become threatened with extinction.

No Uncertain Terms: Most of us have a general idea of what an endangered, threatened, or extinct species is, but biologists have certain definitions for each. In general, an *endangered* species is one that's in immediate danger of becoming extinct. Its numbers are usually low, and it needs protection in order to survive. The giant panda, the whooping crane, the green pitcher plant, and thousands of other plants and animals throughout the world are endangered.

Threatened species—the chimpanzee, the African elephant, the eastern indigo snake, and many others—are those species whose populations aren't yet low enough to be in immediate danger of extinction. They face serious problems, though, and are likely to become endangered if the problems affecting them don't let up. (For more about the problems facing endangered and threatened species, see pages 19-21 and 34-36.)

Extinct species are no longer living. The *Stegosaurus,* the dodo, and the passenger pigeon are examples of extinct species.

A Natural Process: Extinction is not a recent phenomenon. When you look at the history of life on Earth, it's clear that extinction has always been part of the natural evolutionary process. As one group of plants or animals became extinct, for example, others often evolved. The "new" organisms may have outcompeted the "old" ones with more efficient hunting skills, better defense tactics, or any number of other advantages.

Natural disasters and major environmental changes, such as volcanic eruptions or shifts in the climate, also caused extinctions. And sometimes die-offs occurred on a massive scale, with hundreds or even thousands of species disappearing over a period of only a few million years (a short time, geologically). For example, the dinosaurs and many of their contemporaries were casualties of a mass extinction that occurred some 65 million years ago.

Extinction on the Rise: Although extinctions have been occurring naturally for hundreds of millions of years, the current *rate* of extinction is something new. Scientists estimate that the total number of species lost each year may climb to 40,000 by the year 2000, a rate far exceeding any in the last 65 million years.

This accelerated rate of extinction is directly linked to the human population explosion. The number of people on Earth has reached a phenomenal level—from fewer than one billion in 1600, for example, to about five billion today. And scientists estimate that there will probably be over six billion of us by the turn of the century. (For more about the human population explosion, see "The People Factor" on page 13.)

Politics, People, and Endangered Species: What's the connection between endangered species and the rising human population? Many of the problems are pretty obvious. For example, more people take up more space—with their homes, shopping centers, farms, grazing lands, and so on—and that means less living space for those species that can't adapt to changing conditions. People also alter or destroy habitat to get lumber, minerals, oil, and other products from the land. Pollution, illegal and excessive wildlife trade, introduced species, and other people-related problems also take their toll. (For more about these problems, see pages 34-36.)

But the problems people create for other species are not always so obvious. Because the human world is parceled into separate nations, each with different priorities and interests, there are a variety of political, social, and economic crises that affect all species. For example, in some countries where the standard of living is very low, endangered species are usually not a priority. Yet many of these developing nations have many threatened and endangered species that need help to survive.

To add to the problem, many multinational corporations and others exploit the resources in these less-developed countries. And government policies in affluent nations often support environmentally unsound practices abroad.

Worth the Effort: Although many people agree that the rising human population is pushing more and more plants and animals toward extinction, not everyone agrees on just how important it is to slow down the trend—especially considering that it can be very expensive and time-consuming to keep certain endangered plants or animals from becoming extinct, and there are never any guarantees that the efforts will be successful. But there are a lot of important reasons for helping endangered species recover and for preventing plants and animals from ever becoming threatened or endangered in the first place. Here are just a few:

A Moral Obligation—To some, the fact that people are responsible for the possible extinction of so many animals and plants is reason enough to save species from extinction. Each species represents thousands or even millions of years of evolution—but humans have the ability to wipe out such complex evolutionary "designs" almost overnight. Many people question whether this ability to abruptly "interrupt" evolution by causing so many extinctions gives us the right to do so. They feel that, as the source of the problems so many species face, we are morally obligated to do everything we can to help endangered plants and animals recover.

We're All in This Together—The vitality of Earth is reflected in the variety of its inhabitants. So many species being in trouble is a sign that the planet isn't as healthy as it could be. The more successful we are at maintaining or improving the living conditions of as many organisms as possible, the better our chances will be of maintaining or improving the quality of all species' lives on Earth (humans included).

We Can't Afford to Lose Them—The 30 million or more species of plants and animals living in the world today represent more than just a big number. They also represent an incredible variety of life forms. Within the three and one-half billion years or so that life has existed on Earth, animals and plants have evolved into millions of different shapes and sizes, developed a wide range of behaviors, and taken up residence in every type of habitat on the planet.

This biological diversity has been extremely important to people in many different ways. Thousands of different kinds of plants and animals, for example, have been the sources of medicines used in treating cancer, heart disease, and other illnesses. And by cross-breeding wild plants with domestic ones, scientists have bred disease-resistant food crops that have improved and revitalized older, more vulnerable strains. The diversity of plants and animals has also been the source of a lot of the products we use every day: fibers, paper, and plastics, to name a few.

Free Services—Biological diversity provides us with much more than products, though. It also provides us with a variety of special "ecosystem services," such as clean water, a breathable atmosphere, and natural climate control.

For example, as water cycles through a natural community, the plants and animals that live there continually add waste materials to the water. But decomposers in the community continually clean up the waste material by breaking it down into nutrients and incorporating them into their own bodies. This complex interaction of plants, animals, and microorganisms maintains a constant supply of fresh water on the planet. Tampering with this complex system by eliminating certain plant and animal species could have serious consequences for worldwide water quality. Plants, animals, and microorganisms also help remove natural and people-made wastes from the air, help prevent erosion and flooding, and help maintain the balance of carbon dioxide in the atmosphere.

The Spice of Life: Preserving the diversity that has given us so much (and can continue to do so) is, in most scientists' view, the principal reason for slowing the rate of extinction we've set in motion. Since most of the species that are estimated to become extinct each year are probably animals and plants that have never been identified, described, or cataloged, we don't even know what we're losing. Many people feel that every time we lose a species, the world becomes a poorer place—and that the loss of diversity will ultimately make our own lives poorer too.

Darwin's rhea

Leonard Lee Rue IV

Grevy's zebra

Leonard Lee Rue III

Endangered Species ABCs

Make an ABC book of endangered and threatened plants and animals and recite a short rhyme.

Objective:
Describe several threatened and endangered plants and animals.

Ages:
Primary

Materials:
- **copies of pages 16 and 17**
- **construction paper or writing paper**
- **glue**
- **markers or crayons**
- **copies of the rhyme below**
- **paper punches**
- **yarn**
- **scissors**

Subject:
Science

 undreds of plants and animals around the world are threatened with extinction. In this alphabet activity, you can introduce your kids to the variety of wildlife that is in danger of becoming extinct.

Begin by passing out copies of pages 16 and 17 to each person, along with 13 sheets of paper. Also provide glue, scissors, markers or crayons, paper punches, and yarn. Explain that the plants and animals pictured are either threatened or endangered. Discuss what these words mean using the information on page 3. Also explain that not all turtles, butterflies, snails, etc., are in trouble—but the kinds shown are. (See "What's What" on page 27 for more about each of the plants and animals shown.) Then have the kids color the plant and animal pictures, cut them out, and use them to make an alphabet book by following these directions:

1. Fold the sheets of paper in half, making a booklet with 26 pages.
2. Punch two holes along the fold of the booklet, doing a few pages at a time, and tie the pages together with yarn.
3. Glue each picture to a page, putting the pictures in alphabetical order (see diagram).

Once the kids have made their booklets, tell them to draw the first letter of the plant or animal's name next to each picture. Then go through the plant and animal names as a group, helping the kids learn how to pronounce each one. For older primary children, pass out the simple rhyme below and have the kids copy each rhyme underneath the appropriate picture. Afterward, go through the rhyme as a group.

Note: The only letter without an animal or plant is X. You can have the kids skip that letter or use that page to draw a picture of an extinct plant or animal and write the word *extinct* next to it.

Rhyme:

A is for Aye-Aye,
With its strange little hands.
B is for Butterfly,
From faraway lands.

C is for Cactus,
As prickly as can be.
D is for Dugong,
A big beast of the sea.

E is for Eagle,
With strong talons and beak.
F is for Ferret,
So slender and sleek.

G is for Gavial,
It has quite a snout.
H is for Hyena,
It can bark, growl, and shout.

I is for Indri,
With eyes big and bright.
J is for Jaguar,
This cat hunts at night.

K is for Kakapo,
This strange parrot can glide.
L is for Leopard,
It has spots on its hide.

M is for Mandrill,
Its colors are bright.
N is for Numbat,
It's brown-and-white striped.

O is for Orchid,
A plant that's quite rare.
P is for Pitcher Plant,
Fly trappers with hair.

Q is for Quetzal,
Green, crimson, and blue.
R is for Rhea,
It can run faster than you.

S is for Snail,
This kind lives in the trees.
T is for Turtle,
This one swims in the seas.

U is for Urial,
It's a sheep, not a goat.
V is for Vicuña,
It has a fuzzy, thick coat.

W is for Whale,
This sea mammal breathes air.
Y is for Yak,
It has long, shaggy hair.

Z is for Zebra,
It's last on the list.
Now the rhyme's over—
Which letter was missed?

A is for aye-aye, with its strange little hands.

Get the Connection!

Take part in an opinion poll and discuss the ecological importance of all species.

Objectives:
Discuss why people value some living things more than others. Explain why all plants and animals are ecologically important.

Ages:
Intermediate and Advanced

Materials:
- *copies of the opinion poll below*
- *pencils*
- *chalkboard or easel paper*
- *art supplies*
- *reference books (optional)*

Subject:
Science

California condor   Los Angeles Zoo

Many people are familiar with the plight of the giant panda. But not many people know much, if anything, about the plight of the green pitcher plant. Although both are endangered species, the panda gets a lot more press than the pitcher plant. In this two-part activity, your kids can explore their own feelings about how they value different species and then discuss whether it's important to protect all species—even the ones that aren't so "famous."

PART 1: EVERYTHING COUNTS

Before starting, make enough copies of "What Do You Think?" below for everyone in your group. Then pass out a copy to each child and go over the questions with the kids. (Make sure they're familiar, at least in a general way, with all of the animals listed in question #5. For example, explain that a California condor is a vulture-like bird with a 10-foot [3-m] wingspan.) Then tell the kids that they should read each question carefully on their own and answer it according to how they feel.

When the kids have finished the opinion poll, summarize their responses on a chalkboard or piece of easel paper. Then discuss the opinion poll using the information under "What's Important?"

(continued next page)

WHAT DO YOU THINK?

1. Which do you think it's more important to save: endangered plants or endangered animals? Why?
2. Your town is thinking about building a recreation center in your neighborhood. But the proposed site is the home of an endangered insect, and building the center might wipe out the insect. Do you think it's OK for the recreation center to be built on that site? Explain your answer.
3. Would you feel different if there were an endangered bird living on the site where the center might be built? Why or why not?
4. Which of the following do you think it's most important to save?
   a. animals that are very beautiful
   b. large animals, such as whales, giant pandas, and grizzly bears
   c. all types of animals
   d. animals that provide people with food or clothing
   e. animals that live in the United States

5. You have just been put in charge of a team that will be working to save the 10 endangered species listed below. But you have only enough money and materials to work with one species at a time. Number the plants and animals in the order you would try to save them, with #1 being the most important species to save. What other information would you need to make your decision?
   ___ cheetah
   ___ California condor
   ___ mission blue butterfly
   ___ salt marsh harvest mouse
   ___ red wolf
   ___ gray bat
   ___ pygmy rattlesnake
   ___ lady slipper orchid
   ___ bald eagle
   ___ giant panda

apple tree
bamboo
dung beetle
earthworm
grasshopper
oak tree
penicillin mold
plankton
salmon

PART 2: WHAT'S IMPORTANT?

After tallying up the results, discuss why some people are often more interested in protecting birds and mammals than reptiles, amphibians, insects and other "lower" animals, and plants. Also talk about why people are more likely to want to protect large and/or beautiful species than smaller, less beautiful ones. For example, most people would probably support a panda protection program over a mouse or beetle protection program. (Some people feel that smaller animals aren't as important as larger species. Some people also feel that mammals and birds are more important than insects, reptiles, and other animals. Another feeling is that animals are more important than plants. Point out that all living things depend on plants for food, homes, and many other "services." You might also mention that many people tend to place more importance on species that are pretty, cute, or cuddly-looking.)

Explain that despite people's opinions, all species of plants, animals, and microorganisms are important in a natural community. (You might want to point out that even though all species are important, scientists often have to set priorities based on time constraints, money limitations, and other factors.) To emphasize the ecological importance of all species, no matter how unattractive or small, use krill as an example. Describe how krill, a tiny shrimplike crustacean (see diagram), is critical to the survival of many other species. Explain that billions of these tiny creatures live in Antarctic waters and provide food for seals, squid, fish, penguins, baleen whales, and many other types of animals.

Then divide the group into several teams and give each team the same challenge: They must show how one small or not-so-glamorous animal, plant, or microorganism is important to people and/or a natural community. Give the teams research time and explain that they can write reports, draw diagrams, make murals, or do a combination of projects to illustrate how their individual plant, animal, or microorganism is important. (See the list in the margin for examples.)

As a wrap-up, tell each of the kids to have one or two adults fill out the original opinion poll. Then compare the results of the adult answers to the group's and discuss ways to educate people about the importance of all species.

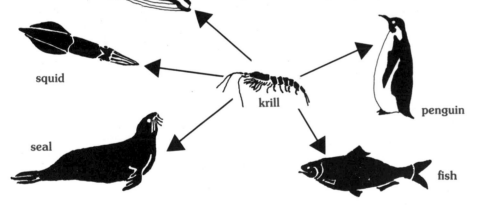

whale

squid

krill

seal

penguin

fish

The Rare Scare

Compare several imaginary animals to determine which has the characteristics of a "typical" endangered species.

Objectives:
Define endangered, threatened, and extinct. Describe several characteristics that make an animal extremely susceptible to extinction.

Rhinoceroses, pandas, condors, and many other endangered species have more in common than just their endangered status. Many share characteristics that make them extremely susceptible to becoming extinct. Start off this activity by passing out a copy of page 15 to each person. Explain that each of these animals is imaginary, but each has characteristics that are similar to those of real animals living today. Have the kids read the information given for each animal, then have them decide which of the animals would be the first to become extinct as more and more people move into the area where each animal lives.

After each person has picked an animal, take a tally to see how many kids voted for each animal. Ask the kids why they picked these animals. Then explain that many animals that are threatened or endangered share one or more characteristics that make them more prone to

Ages:
Intermediate

Materials:
- *copies of page 15*
- *index cards*
- *markers*
- *easel paper or chalkboard*

Subject:
Science

extinction. Discuss some of these characteristics, using the information below. After the discussion, have the kids look at page 15 again to see if they agree with their original choices. Then take another tally and compare the results to those of the first one.

Explain that the crested crabbit is the animal that will probably become extinct first because it has so many of the characteristics that make an animal susceptible to extinction. For example, it has a very limited range, has a low birth rate, has a very specialized diet, migrates, and nests in only one type of tree. Explain that animals that have one or more of these characteristics usually do fine until people-related problems, such as habitat loss and pollution, start to affect them.

ANIMALS ARE MORE PRONE TO EXTINCTION IF THEY . . .

INTERFERE IN SOME WAY WITH PEOPLE'S ACTIVITIES:
Explain that some animals may kill livestock, eat or ruin crops, or feed on animals that people also like to eat. And because they interfere with people's activities, these animals are often shot, poisoned, or harmed in some other way. Ask the kids if they can think of some examples. (many predators, such as eagles, wolves, jaguars, and tigers, as well as geese, ducks, and other birds that sometimes eat crops)

MIGRATE:
Animals that migrate usually depend on several different habitat areas. Because of this, they can be very vulnerable to habitat destruction. For example, many songbirds that migrate to tropical forests in winter are in trouble because thousands of acres of their rain forest habitat have been developed into pastures, farms, towns, and roads.

HAVE VERY SPECIFIC FOOD OR NESTING REQUIREMENTS:
Some animals are super "picky" about what they eat or where they live, or both. These specialized animals, which are often adapted to eating only one type of food or living in only one type of area, can become endangered if their food source or nesting site disappears. For example, the Delmarva fox squirrel once thrived in the open forests that grew along the Eastern Shore of Maryland, Virginia, and Delaware. As more and more of these forests disappeared, so did the squirrels. And today the Delmarva fox squirrel is listed as an endangered species.

ARE VERY SENSITIVE TO CHANGES:
Many animals have a very difficult time adapting to changes in their environment. For example, birds of prey and many other animals are very sensitive to chemical changes in their environment, such as the introduction of pesticides. Other animals have a hard time competing with introduced species that have the same nesting or food requirements. For example, bluebirds—a species native to North America—have a hard time competing for nesting sites with starlings, which were introduced from Europe in the early 1900s.

HAVE SMALL BROODS AND LONG GESTATION PERIODS:
Ask the kids if they can think of some animals that give birth to only one or two young every year or every two or three years. (elephants, bats, condors, and so on) Explain that when the populations of these animals drop, it takes much more time for their populations to recover because of the low birth rate. And the animals sometimes become extinct before they have time to make a comeback.

Animals with low birth rates have another problem too: They don't reproduce fast enough to produce offspring that can adapt to changing conditions. Have the kids compare the reproductive capabilities of an elephant with those of a cockroach. Explain that on the average, an elephant has about three young every 10 years and that a cockroach has 80 young every half year. Copy the following figures on the board and explain that if all the animals lived and mated, here's the number of young produced in each generation.

Note: These figures are simplified and represent approximate numbers of individuals per generation.

Elephant	Cockroach
1st Generation	
3	80
2nd Generation	
6	3362
3rd Generation	
13	137,842
4th Generation	
28	5,651,522
5th Generation	
61	231,712,403
6th Generation	
132	9,500,208,482

Ask the kids to compare the number of years it takes an elephant and a cockroach to produce a 6th generation. (Since an elephant has an average of 3 young every 10 years, and a cockroach has an average of 80 young every half year, it would take elephants 60 years to produce 6 generations, and only 3 years for the cockroaches to do the same.) Emphasize that because of their high birth rate, cockroaches have more opportunities to adapt to changes in their environment.

ARE NATURALLY RARE:
Some animals are rare throughout their range, and others have a very limited range. In both cases, the animals are often vulnerable to habitat destruction and other people-caused problems. For example, many of the native plants and animals that live on the islands of Hawaii are naturally rare. And as more people move into the area, many of these already rare plants and animals face habitat loss, competition from introduced species, new diseases, and other problems.

(continued next page)

To demonstrate why specialized animals are often more susceptible to extinction, play this action game outside. Before starting, make a set of food cards by drawing the symbols and words, shown in the chart below, on index cards. For a group of 30 kids, you should make 10 fruit, 15 leaves, 15 insects, 10 small mammals and reptiles, 10 birds and eggs, and 10 snails.

Also copy the chart on a chalkboard or piece of easel paper so the kids can see which symbol stands for which food items and which foods each team eats. Before going outside, divide the group into five teams and give each team a number. Then tell them to look at the chart to see what they eat. For example, the kids in Team #1 are animals that eat fruit, leaves, insects, small mammals and reptiles, birds and eggs, and snails. And the kids in Team #2 are animals that feed on insects, small mammals and reptiles, eggs, and snails.

Now go outside and spread the food cards in a large playing area. (It's a good idea to play this game only on non-windy days.) Remind the kids what each team can eat and what each card represents. Then have the kids form a huge circle around the playing area. When you say "go," have the kids get down on their hands and knees and crawl around the playing circle to find food. (If the ground is wet or muddy, have the kids hop instead of crawl.) Tell them to collect as many food cards as they can find, but that they should collect only the type of food they can eat. For example, the kids in team #4 would be able to collect only insects, leaves, and fruit.

After all the cards have been collected, have the kids count how many they have. Explain that to survive, each animal needs at least two food cards. How many animals didn't find enough food?

Now play again, but explain that people have destroyed much of the habitat in the area to build an airport, shopping mall, and housing complex. Take away five of each type of food card and scatter the cards again. Which animals survived the second time? Ask the kids which animals had the hardest time surviving and why. (The animals in team #5 probably had the hardest time because they had the most specialized diet and when their food source became depleted, they would have starved. The non-specialized eaters, on the other hand, could eat another type of food when one of their food sources became depleted.) Finally, point out other examples of animals living in North America that have very specialized food or nesting requirements. (Snail kites feed on only one type of snail, Kirtland's warblers nest only in jack pines, red-cockaded woodpeckers nest only in old-growth forests, black-footed ferrets feed mainly on prairie dogs, and so on.)

TEAM #	Fruit	Leaves	Insects	Small mammals and reptiles	Birds and eggs	Snails
1	X	X	X	X	X	X
2			X	X	X	X
3	X	X				
4	X	X	X			X
5						X

A Timely Activity

Make a time line that shows some famous (and infamous) events in conservation history.

Objectives:
Name several species that have become extinct since the 1600s and discuss why they died out. Talk about some of the steps people have taken to protect animals, plants, and their habitats.

Ages:
Intermediate

Materials:
- *copy of page 12*
- *crepe paper party streamers*
- *tape*
- *reference books*
- *drawing paper*
- *writing paper*
- *scissors*
- *markers or paints*
- *glue*

Subjects:
Science and History

The year 1914 is infamous in conservation history. That's when a passenger pigeon named Martha died at the Cincinnati Zoo, signaling the extinction of a species that once numbered in the hundreds of millions. If the passenger pigeon hadn't faced extinction until much later in the century—the early 1970s, for example—it might have stood a much better chance of surviving: The Endangered Species Act, passed in 1973, would have mandated an effort to help the passenger pigeon survive.

This activity will help your kids learn about some important events that reflect both the positive and negative aspects of people's relationships with the natural world. It's a good way for kids to learn about some of the species that have become extinct, and it will give them a perspective on what happened when. It will also point out some of the steps people have taken to help species that are in trouble.

To start the activity, make a copy of page 12 and cut apart the "milestones." Then give one milestone to each person. (Depending on the size of your group, you

may want to have some of the kids work in pairs on certain events.) Explain that everyone should find out as much as possible about his or her event and the circumstances that surrounded it. For example, the person who picked the extinction of the dodo bird could find out where the dodo lived, what it looked like, a little about its biology, and why the dodo became extinct. (Encourage the kids to "dig" for facts by using the *Reader's Guide to Periodical Literature*, reference books, and other sources of information.)

When the kids have finished their research, have them make a time line banner by taping a party streamer across the walls. (They may need to tape several streamers together to make the banner stretch around the room.) Then pass out large sheets of drawing paper, markers or paints, and writing paper and have the kids draw or write about their events. Also have some of the kids copy the events listed under "Other Happenings" on separate pieces of paper. Make sure everyone labels his or her picture or pictures. (For example, the person who worked on the dodo could write, "Early 1680s: Extinction of the Dodo Bird.")

Now have the kids tape or glue their drawings chronologically along the time line banner. They should also mark off equal distances for each century and label them. To wrap up the activity, discuss why there are so many events at the "recent" end of the time line. Explain that, for one thing, the number of animals that have become threatened, endangered, or extinct has increased as the human population has expanded. (See page 13 for more about the expanding human population and its effects on other species.) Also, people's increasing understanding of the human-caused problems other species are facing has gradually resulted in laws and other measures designed to protect animals, plants, and their habitats.

(continued next page)

1972: WWF LAUNCHED PROJECT TIGER

1979: 100 PEREGRINE FALCONS RAISED IN CAPTIVITY WERE RELEASED INTO THE WILD.

MILESTONES

Mid 1600s: Elephant birds became extinct.

Early 1680s: Dodo birds became extinct.

1768: Steller's sea cow became extinct.

1782: Bald eagle became national symbol of the United States.

1844: Great auk became extinct.

1872: Yellowstone National Park was established.

1904: Last flock of Carolina parakeets was seen in the wild.

1914: Martha, the last passenger pigeon, died in the Cincinnati Zoo.

1916: The U.S. National Park Service was established.

1945: The whooping crane population reached a low of 19 birds.

1949: Eleven-year-old Glenn Allen started a campaign to save Florida's tiny key deer.

1957: The aye-aye, an unusual primate once thought to be extinct, was rediscovered in Madagascar.

1962: *Silent Spring,* Rachel Carson's book about harmful pesticides, was published.

1972: DDT was banned from most uses in the United States.

1973: The Endangered Species Act was passed.

1979: One hundred peregrine falcons, raised in captivity at Cornell University, were released into parts of their former range.

1981: A small population of black-footed ferrets was discovered in Wyoming. Until then, scientists feared the ferrets had become extinct. The black-footed ferret is one of the rarest mammals in North America.

1982: The International Whaling Commission voted to enact a temporary halt on commercial whaling.

1985: Ivory-billed woodpeckers were seen in Cuba.

OTHER HAPPENINGS

1860s: "Buffalo Bill" Cody killed approximately 4300 American bison in an 18-month period.

1870s: Passengers traveling west by train often shot bison for sport from train windows.

1875: The last-known Labrador duck was shot on Long Island, New York. These ducks lived in the northeastern United States. Market hunting was the main reason they became extinct.

1878: Quaggas became extinct in the wild. Quaggas were zebralike animals that lived in southern Africa. They were killed off mainly by settlers who felt the animals competed with livestock for grazing land.

1878: The last huge nesting of passenger pigeons occurred in a Michigan forest. Millions of these birds nested in an area covering about 100,000 acres (40,000 ha). That's an area bigger than the city of Detroit!

1883: The last captive quagga died in the Amsterdam Zoo.

1894: The sea mink, a weasel-like animal that lived along the coast from Newfoundland to Massachusetts, became extinct. It was hunted for its fur.

Late 1800s and early 1900s: The United States and Canada passed laws to protect bison. Only a few small herds were left by this time.

1900: The Lacey Act was passed. It put an end to the hunting of egrets and other birds whose feathers were used to decorate women's hats.

1903: President Theodore Roosevelt established Pelican Island off the east coast of Florida as the first wildlife refuge in the United States.

1918: The Migratory Bird Treaty Act was passed. This law prohibited the hunting or capture of migratory birds except during hunting season or unless a special permit was obtained.

1932: The last heath hen was spotted on Martha's Vineyard. Heath hens were large, chickenlike birds. They were hunted for their meat.

1940: The Bald Eagle Protection Act was passed.

1950s: Last confirmed sightings of the ivory-billed woodpecker in the United States.

1971: The United States stopped participating in commercial whaling.

1972: The Marine Mammal Protection Act was passed. This law protected all marine mammals in U.S. waters from harassment, hunting, capture, or killing.

1972: Project Tiger was launched by World Wildlife Fund in an effort to save the Indian tiger.

1973: Wildlife officials arrested a ring of fur smugglers. The smugglers had been buying and selling the pelts of endangered and threatened animals for more than a year and a half. They had smuggled more than 99,000 pelts.

1975: CITES (Convention on International Trade in Endangered Species of Wild Fauna and Flora) was ratified by the United States and other nations. CITES regulates international trade in wild animals and plants. More than 90 countries have agreed to follow the guidelines of CITES.

1979: An illegal shipment of the pelts of more than 900 rare and endangered cats was seized in Hong Kong. The pelts had been shipped from Africa in a container labeled "mink."

1981: Wildlife officials made several arrests in a case involving the illegal sale of about 10,000 reptiles.

1984: By this year, the human population had more than quadrupled since 1850.

2000: The world's human population is expected to reach six billion by this time.

The People Factor

Graph human population increases and the number of birds and mammals that have recently become extinct.

Objectives:
Describe several ways that human population growth affects wildlife. Relate human population growth to the increased number of extinct birds and mammals.

Ages:
Intermediate and Advanced

Materials:
- *copies of page 18*
- *markers*
- *graph paper*
- *pencils*
- *drawing paper*
- *rulers*
- *reference books (optional)*
- *copies of pages 16 and 17 (optional)*

Subjects:
Science, Social Studies, and Math

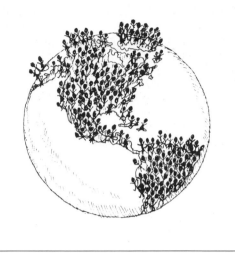

In the last 35 years, the number of people in the world has almost doubled, from 2.6 billion to 5 billion. And scientists estimate that by the year 2100 it could climb to over 10 billion! What does an "exploding" human population have to do with endangered species? Plenty! In this two-part activity, your kids will learn about some of the ways that the growing human population affects plant and animal species around the world, both directly and indirectly.

PART 1: CLOSE TO HOME

Start off the activity by passing out copies of page 18. Have the kids look at the information in the first graph. Ask if anyone can explain what the graph shows. (It shows how the population of the United States has grown since 1800.) Then have the kids look at the information in charts #1 and #2. These charts show the average number of pounds of trash generated by a U.S. citizen each day in 1960, 1970, 1980, and 1986, and the approximate acreage of urban land in the United States. Ask the kids to think about the connection between the information in the charts and the graph of the United States' rising population. (More people use more resources, including energy, food, water, and so on; more people generate more waste, which takes up space [landfills, etc.] and can pollute the environment; more people clear more land to make room for houses, roads, shopping malls, and other development.)

Now have the kids look at the information in chart #3. It shows the number of birds and mammals that have become extinct in the United States and Canada since 1700. Explain that this is an approximate number of extinctions, since no one knows for sure what might have become extinct early in our history. Discuss, in general, the connection between the number of birds and mammals that have become extinct in the United States and the rising human population. (More people, using more resources, settling in new areas, and clearing more land for development, can directly and indirectly harm plant and animal populations. For example, some animals, such as some honeycreepers, have become extinct because of habitat loss and habitat changes. Others, such as passenger pigeons and great auks, have become extinct because of unregulated market hunting. And many have become extinct for a combination of reasons, most stemming from human-related pressures that increase as the human population increases. See pages 19-21 and 34-36 for more about the reasons plants and animals become endangered and extinct.)

(continued next page)

PART 2: A WORLD FULL OF PEOPLE

After discussing some of the effects of the growing U.S. population, have the kids focus on the world population. Explain that in many parts of the world, especially in many Asian, South American, and African countries, the human population is growing even faster than it is in the United States. Tell them to look at the information in chart #4. Explain that this represents the world's population growth since 1650. Pass out a large piece of graph paper, along with rulers, pencils, and markers. Then tell the kids to make a line graph on the left-hand side of their papers showing the population of the world. Tell them the vertical axis can represent the human population in millions and the horizontal axis can represent the years.

Now have the kids look at the information in chart #5. Explain that this information shows the approximate number of species of birds and mammals that have become extinct around the world since 1600. Have the kids use this information to make a bar graph next to the population graph they just made. You can suggest that they use one color to represent birds and another color to represent mammals. (Older children can try to combine both sets of data in the same graph by making the right vertical axis represent the number of species that have become extinct. See diagram below.)

When the kids have finished graphing, discuss how the growing human population is threatening many of the world's plants and animals. Explain that the number of plants and animals becoming endangered is rising every year, and as the world's population continues to grow, people will continue to put more pressure on plant and animal species.

Afterward, have each of the kids draw a picture of an extinct animal. (See the list of extinct animals in the margin.) Tell them to research the animals to find out why they became extinct, then have them write a sentence or two about each animal under its picture. You might also want to pass out copies of pages 16 and 17 to show the kids pictures of animals and plants that are in trouble today.

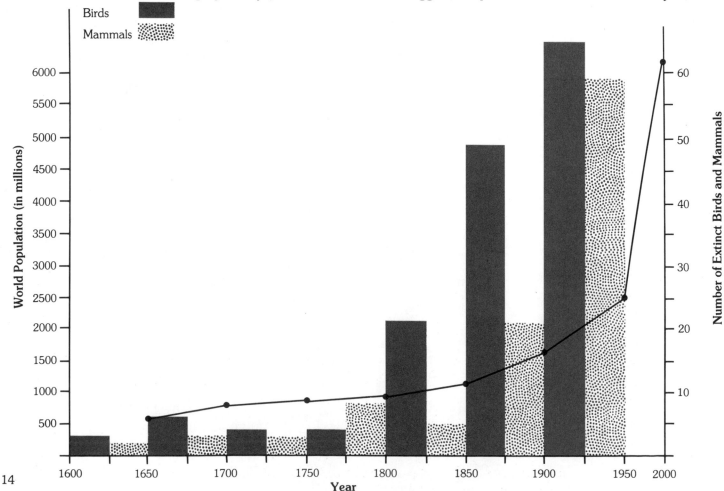

14

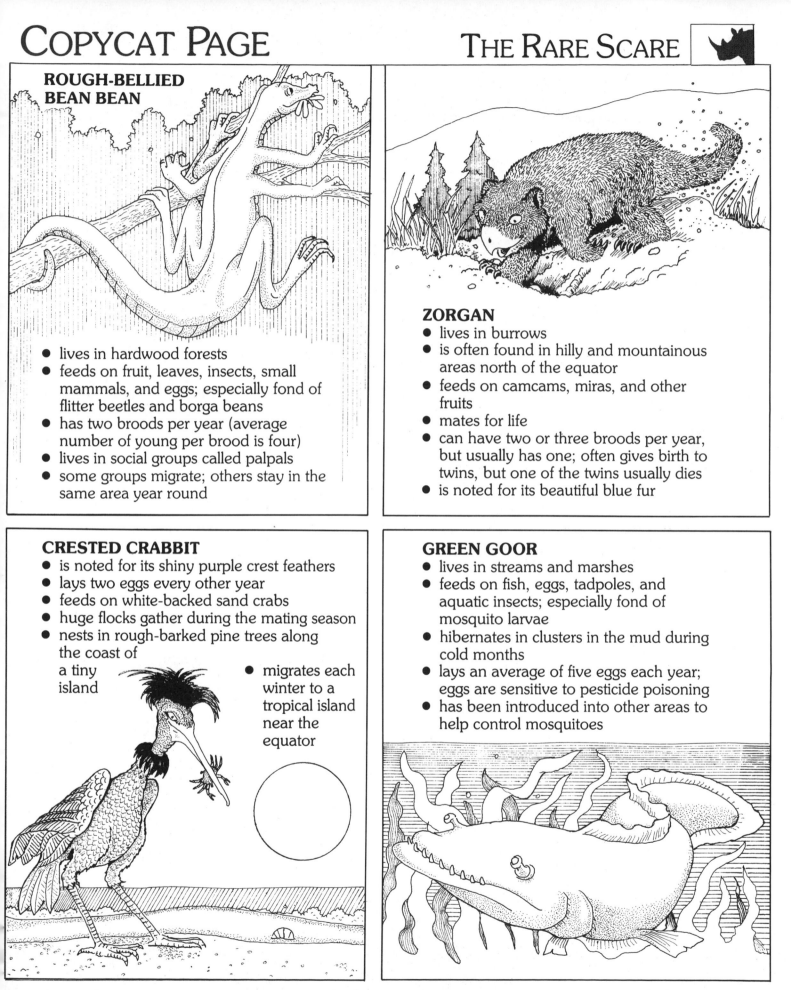

ROUGH-BELLIED BEAN BEAN

- lives in hardwood forests
- feeds on fruit, leaves, insects, small mammals, and eggs; especially fond of flitter beetles and borga beans
- has two broods per year (average number of young per brood is four)
- lives in social groups called palpals
- some groups migrate; others stay in the same area year round

ZORGAN

- lives in burrows
- is often found in hilly and mountainous areas north of the equator
- feeds on camcams, miras, and other fruits
- mates for life
- can have two or three broods per year, but usually has one; often gives birth to twins, but one of the twins usually dies
- is noted for its beautiful blue fur

CRESTED CRABBIT

- is noted for its shiny purple crest feathers
- lays two eggs every other year
- feeds on white-backed sand crabs
- huge flocks gather during the mating season
- nests in rough-barked pine trees along the coast of a tiny island
- migrates each winter to a tropical island near the equator

GREEN GOOR

- lives in streams and marshes
- feeds on fish, eggs, tadpoles, and aquatic insects; especially fond of mosquito larvae
- hibernates in clusters in the mud during cold months
- lays an average of five eggs each year; eggs are sensitive to pesticide poisoning
- has been introduced into other areas to help control mosquitoes

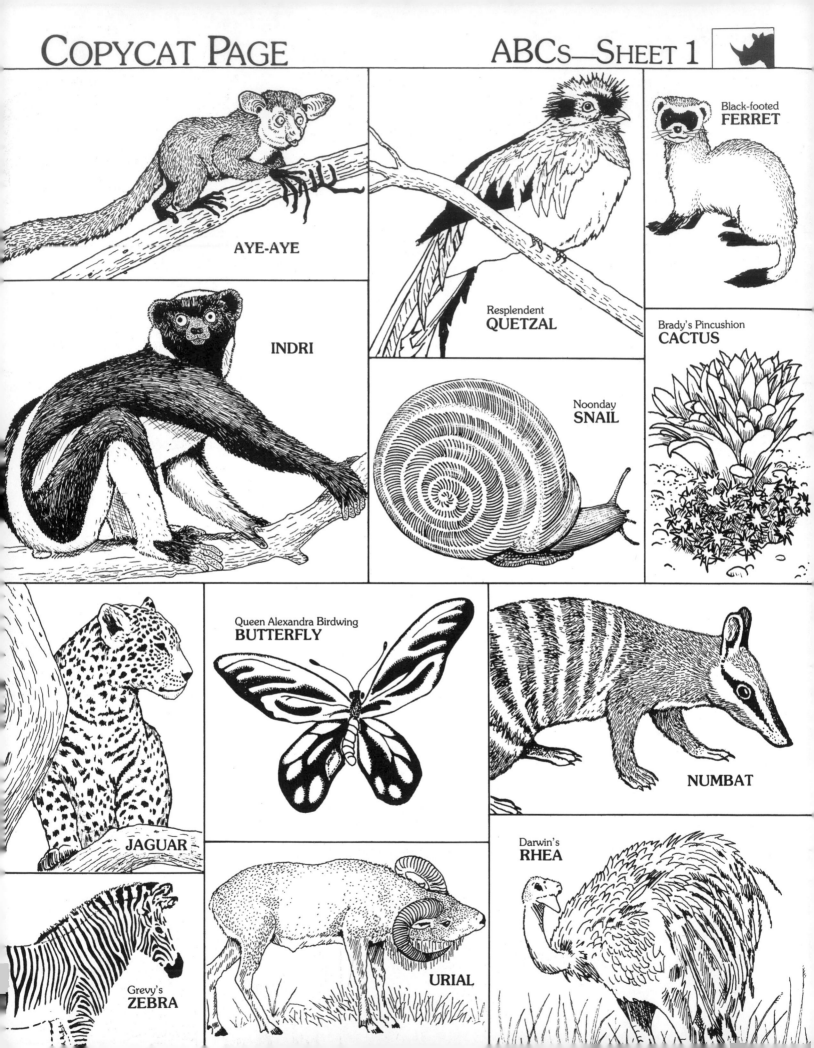

AYE-AYE

Resplendent
QUETZAL

Black-footed
FERRET

INDRI

Noonday
SNAIL

Brady's Pincushion
CACTUS

JAGUAR

Queen Alexandra Birdwing
BUTTERFLY

NUMBAT

Grevy's
ZEBRA

URIAL

Darwin's
RHEA

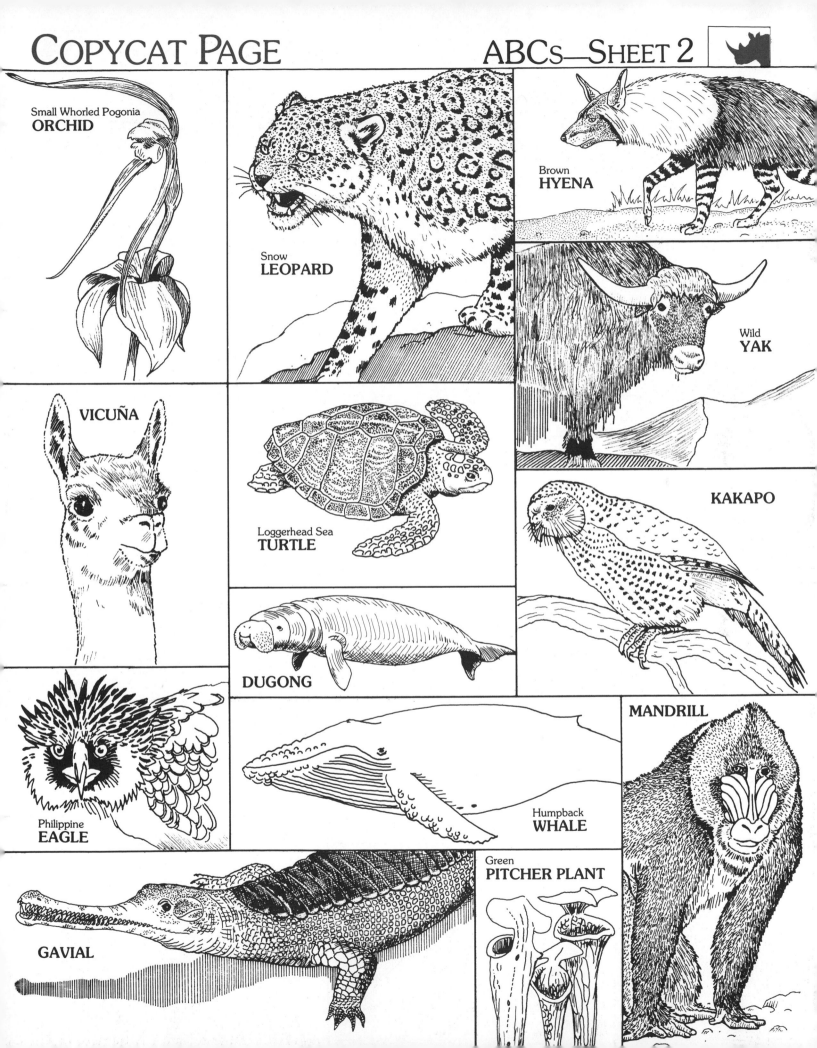

Small Whorled Pogonia
ORCHID

Snow
LEOPARD

Brown
HYENA

Wild
YAK

VICUÑA

Loggerhead Sea
TURTLE

KAKAPO

DUGONG

Philippine
EAGLE

Humpback
WHALE

MANDRILL

GAVIAL

Green
PITCHER PLANT

U.S. Population (1800-1980)

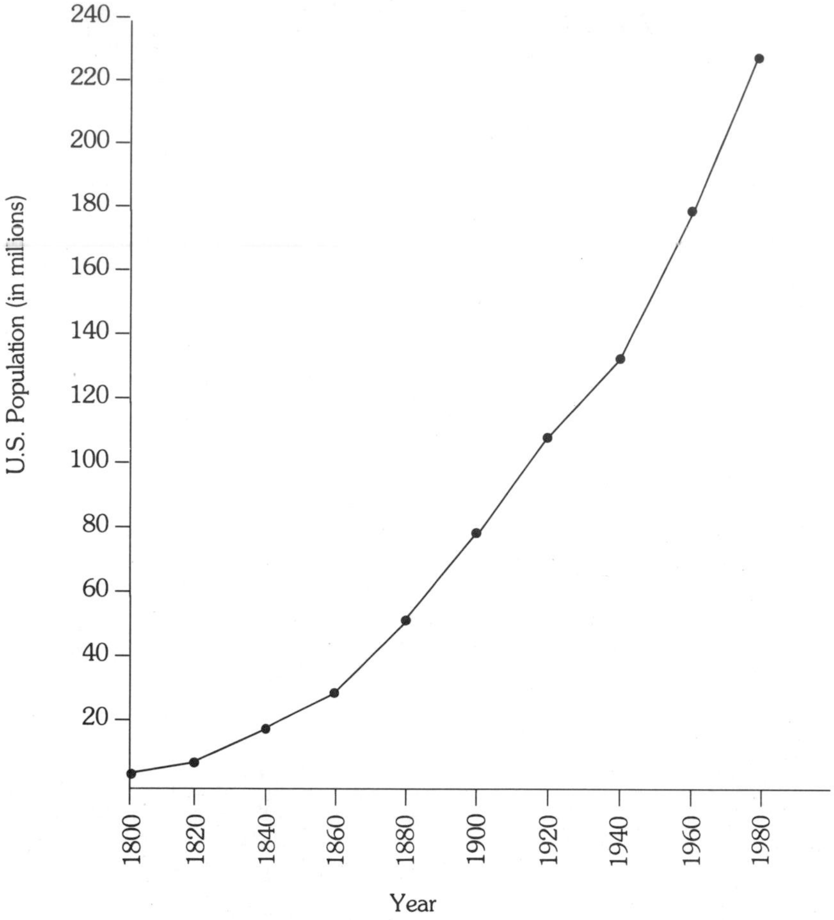

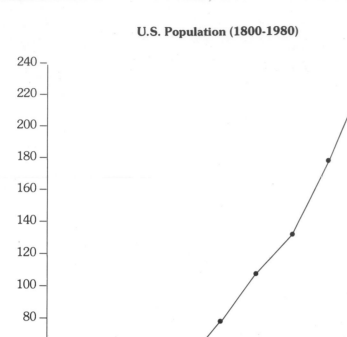

Year

Chart #3

Number of Extinct Birds and Mammals (U.S. and Canada)		
Year	Birds	Mammals
1700-1799	0	2
1800-1899	20	4
1900-1980	19	27

Chart #4

World Population (in millions)	
1650	550
1700	610
1750	760
1800	950
1850	1210
1900	1630
1950	2520
2000	6200

Chart #1

Average Amount of Trash Generated (in lbs/person/day)	
1960	2.6
1970	3.5
1980	3.7
1986	4.5-5

Chart #2

Approximate Number of Acres of Urban Land in the U.S. (in millions of acres)	
1960	25.5
1970	34.6
1980	47.3

Chart #5

Number of Extinct Birds and Mammals (worldwide)		
Year	Birds	Mammals
1600-1649	3	2
1650-1699	6	3
1700-1749	4	3
1750-1799	4	8
1800-1849	22	5
1850-1899	48	22
1900-1949	65	59

THE HABITAT CONNECTION

Every hour, at least 1000 acres (400 ha) of tropical rain forests are destroyed worldwide. Considering that over 50 percent of all species on Earth live in these forests, the enormity of this destruction, in terms of both number of acres and number of plant and animal species, is staggering. But rain forests aren't the only habitats in trouble. Grasslands, deserts, wetlands, temperate forests, coral reefs, estuaries, and most other types of habitats are also disappearing at tremendous rates. This habitat loss is the major reason plant and animal species are becoming threatened, endangered, and extinct. And habitat destruction is considered the single greatest obstacle to helping many endangered species recover.

WILD SPACES ARE VITAL PLACES

It's not surprising that habitat loss is so devastating to wildlife. All animals and plants depend on their habitats for life's necessities, which include food and other nutrients, water, shelter, and living space. The plants and animals within a habitat also depend on each other and interact in many ways to form a balanced, working ecosystem. When people clear a forest, fill in a marsh, or make other habitat changes, they not only destroy plant and animal homes, they also upset a system that has taken years to become established.

Habitat changes affect species in different ways. Some animals and plants, such as pigeons, house sparrows, and dandelions, are super adapters. They seem to thrive in people-created habitats such as abandoned lots, grassy backyards, and city parks. But other species, which aren't as adaptable, have a much tougher time trying to "make it" in a world of pavement and parks. Here's a look at why some plants and animals are more susceptible to habitat loss and how habitat changes affect species in different ways:

A Special Diet: Day after day, snail kites in the Everglades feed on the same thing—apple snails. Like many animals, these birds are super-specialized feeders that rely on only one type of food for the bulk of their diet. Animals like this run into trouble when something happens to their food source. In the case of the snail kite, the problem is wetland destruction. Thousands of acres of wetlands, where the snails live, have been destroyed or altered by people. This wetland loss has caused the snail population to drop drastically, which in turn has caused the kite population to drop too.

Home Sweet Home: Years ago, ivory-billed woodpeckers lived in old-growth, swampy forests in the southern United States. But today, these large woodpeckers are believed to be extinct in the United States. What happened? The ivory-billed woodpeckers relied on the old-growth forests in these swampy areas for food and nesting sites. And as these forests were cut down, the population of woodpeckers declined.

Just like the ivory-billed woodpecker, many animals and plants rely on a specific type of habitat for survival. For example, giant pandas depend on the bamboo forests in the mountains of China, and Delmarva fox squirrels depend on old-growth coastal forests along the Eastern Shore of Virginia, Maryland, and Delaware. Animals and plants with specific habitat needs such as these are extremely susceptible to extinction when changes occur in their habitats. (For more about the

ivory-billed woodpecker

characteristics that make species particularly vulnerable to extinction, see "The Rare Scare" on page 8.)

Restricted Ranges: The problem of habitat loss is especially critical for animals and plants that live in only one place on Earth. El segundo butterflies, for example, live in only a couple of small areas in southern California. And Devil's Hole pupfish live in only one small pool in Death Valley. If people significantly change or destroy the areas where such localized species live, these plants and animals could be doomed to become extinct. In some parts of the world, hundreds of plants and animals live only on a single island, in a remote valley, or in some other restricted area. On Madagascar, for instance, 80 percent of the native flowering plants are found nowhere else in the world. And scientists estimate that many of the species on this tropical island are disappearing every year.

No Place to Go: When some warblers reach their tropical wintering grounds in the fall, they may find that the areas have changed drastically or have disappeared altogether. These birds, like many other animals, migrate between different habitat areas at different times of the year. When people destroy a significant part of either habitat, or if the animals' resting spots along the way are destroyed, many of them may not be able to survive or reproduce. Some scientists worry that tropical de-forestation in Latin America and the Caribbean may be causing the numbers of some songbirds, including many North American species, to drop, since so many winter in these rain forests.

Chopping Up Habitats: People don't have to demolish an entire habitat to leave thousands of animals and plants homeless. Because species adapt to specific conditions in their habitats, even partial destruction can be devastating. When part of a forest is cut down, for example, plants and animals that were in the "middle" of the area may suddenly be at the edge. Increased light, drier air, and predation by "outsiders" may wipe out many of these organisms.

Some habitats aren't just pared down, they're chopped into isolated segments. For example, when a road or housing development separates one part of a forest from another, the plants or animals that were once a single, large population now become small, isolated populations. And this can cause many problems, including inbreeding, which often causes unhealthy traits to be passed along from one generation to the next. It's sometimes hard to determine exactly how much space different species need in order to maintain healthy populations—but scientists think that even some habitat areas that have been preserved specifically for wildlife, such as national parks and wildlife refuges, may not be big enough to fulfill certain animals' needs.

WHERE ARE ALL THE WILD LANDS GOING?

It's not hard to guess that most habitat loss in the world is caused by people. And it's also not hard to guess that much of the wildlife habitat turns into buildings, farms, roads, lakes, and other types of human development. This fast-paced, worldwide destruction not only displaces and destroys many plant and animal species, it also can cause soil erosion and toxic runoff and other types of pollution. For example, in some areas coral reefs have been completely smothered by silt from nearby construction sites.

But this type of development isn't the only cause of habitat loss. Here's a quick look at some of the other reasons wild areas are in trouble:

The Cattle Connection: In the past few decades, thousands of acres of pristine rain forest in Central and South America have been converted into grazing lands for cattle. Although scientists are working on ways to replant the devastated rain forest areas, it's already too late for many of the species that have been displaced.

Cattle, as well as sheep, goats, and other grazing animals, also create another habitat problem—overgrazing. Overgrazing can quickly turn healthy habitats into wastelands. (For more about the effects of overgrazing, see page 46 of *NatureScope—Discovering Deserts* [Vol. 1, No. 5].)

Products for People: Firewood, lumber, gold, coal, oil, and many other valuable products can be found in wild areas. Unfortunately, a lot of land is destroyed or altered in the process of harvesting or mining these materials and in getting them from the wild to the people that buy them. For example, mining not only tears up land where minerals are actually being mined, it also destroys the areas where mining roads are built to get vehicles to and from the mining site. Mining can also cause runoff and soil erosion, and it often opens up remote areas to more development.

Reckless Recreation: Off-road vehicle (ORV) use has become a favorite method of "getting around" for many people in the United States and other countries. Unfortunately, some ORV users often illegally take their vehicles into restricted areas in deserts, wetlands, and other habitats, where they can cause a lot of damage in a very short time. In Kenya, for example, a booming tourist trade brings a flood of visitors to its wildlife parks and reserves each year. And vehicles carrying these tourists—especially in the reserves—don't always stick to designated trails. Instead they travel haphazardly across the land, wearing down the soil and disrupting wildlife.

HOPE FOR HABITATS

It seems inevitable that as the human population explodes into the 21st century, habitat loss will occur at an even greater pace than it has in the past. Yet many people around the world are trying to pull in the reins of runaway habitat destruction. For example, the World Bank and some other financial institutions are beginning to be more selective in the development projects they fund. Several major projects slated for India, Nepal, the Dominican Republic, and other developing countries are being delayed until the risks to the environment are carefully evaluated. And on another front, scientists are working hard to find out more about the habitat needs of particular species, how to recover habitat that has been destroyed, and how people's needs can be balanced with the needs of plant and animal species. (For more about habitat recovery, see "Undoing the Damage" on page 51.)

Although many reports say that current habitat destruction trends cannot be reversed, many people disagree. The scientists, legislators, economists, educators, and other people working to protect habitat believe there is hope, and that working to save habitat is the best thing we can do to save wildlife and ourselves.

Meet a Panda

Make panda masks and interview a panda puppet.

Objectives:
List several reasons why pandas are endangered. Discuss some facts about pandas.

Ages:
Primary

Materials:
- *pencils*
- *writing paper*
- *materials for panda mask and puppet (see page 60)*
- *pictures of giant pandas*
- *map of the world*
- *bamboo (optional)*
- *table or large piece of stiff cardboard (optional)*

Subject:
Science

Luise Woelflein

One of the most appealing animals in the world is the giant panda. It is also one of the most endangered animals. In this activity, your kids will learn more about the panda and its problems, as well as the problems many endangered species face.

Before starting the activity, make a simple panda puppet by following the directions on page 60. Also review the panda facts on the next page to find out about the natural history of the panda and why it is endangered.

Begin by showing the kids pictures of giant pandas and pointing out on a map of the world where these mammals live. Explain that China is the third largest country in the world and it has more people than any other country. Also explain that pandas are one of the world's rarest animals and that the kids will be finding out more about these beautiful creatures by interviewing a panda puppet named Ping-Ling.

First have the kids write down one question they would like to ask a panda if they could. (If the kids are too young to write, have them just think about what they would like to know about pandas.) As the kids are writing their questions, you may want to make a simple stage in the front of the room by turning a table on its side or by using a large piece of stiff cardboard. (You could also draw a simple bamboo forest scene on the cardboard to make the stage a little more realistic.) Then introduce the group to Ping-Ling, the giant panda. You can ad-lib a puppet show, prompting the kids to answer and ask questions and talk to Ping-Ling. Or you can follow a script (see the sample below). You also might want to copy the facts and refer to them during the interview. At the end of the interview, have the kids make their own paper-plate panda masks, following the instructions on page 60.

SAMPLE SCRIPT

Hello, boys and girls. My name is Ping-Ling. Can everyone say *Ping-Ling?* I'm a giant panda.

Does anyone know where giant pandas like me live? That's right, in a country called China.

I live in forests high in the mountains where the weather is often cold and misty . . . *brrrrr.* How do you think I stay warm?

That's right. My thick fur keeps me warm. And it also helps keep me dry. Can you think of something you wear that helps keep you dry?

Just like a raincoat, my fur helps keep water from soaking down into my skin and making me cold. What colors are my fur? Can you think of another animal that has black-and-white fur? (zebra, skunk, etc.)

Has anyone ever seen a panda at the zoo? Pandas get pretty big. Why, I know a panda back in China that's almost six feet tall!

(Hold up a piece of bamboo.) Does anyone know what this is? It's bamboo—my favorite food. In the mountains where I live, there are huge forests of bamboo. And I eat pounds and pounds of bamboo every day to stay healthy. I like the tender young shoots that come up in the spring the best.

And so on . . .

GIANT PANDA FACTS

- Giant pandas are chubby mammals that live in a few remote mountainous regions in China. They have thick fur with bright black-and-white markings.
- A panda's coat acts like a thick winter raincoat. The fur is water-repellent and helps keep a panda warm and dry in cold, wet weather.
- Pandas are plant eaters and they feed mainly on a plant called bamboo. Sometimes pandas eat other types of plants and occasionally they eat small mammals. But pandas usually eat only the stems, twigs, leaves, and fresh young shoots of the different types of bamboo. They especially like the tender shoots of young bamboo plants.
- Bamboo, which is in the grass family, is hard to digest. Some animals, such as cows, have special stomachs to help them digest tough plants. But pandas don't have special stomachs. So to get enough nourishment, a panda has to eat huge amounts of bamboo—22 to 44 pounds (10 to 20 kg)—every day, all year round. And that means most pandas spend about 14 hours a day feeding.
- Many different types of bamboo are found in the mountain forests of China where the pandas live. The bamboo grows in thick bunches and provides food for the pandas throughout the year.
- When pandas aren't eating, they're usually resting. They often just lie down on the ground, wherever they happen to be. In stormy weather, they sometimes try to find a cave or some other type of shelter.

- Some pandas live as long as 30 years and weigh as much as 260 pounds (117 kg). Full-grown pandas are close to 5 feet (1.5 m) tall when standing up and some grow as tall as 5 feet, 8 inches (1.7 m). Males and females look alike, but females are a bit smaller than the males.
- Pandas usually live alone. Each panda lives in an area that's about one to two miles (1.6 to 3.2 km) in diameter. Although pandas will share part of their territory with other pandas, they usually don't get too close to each other.
- In the spring, pandas search for a mate. They mark their territories with special scent glands to let other pandas know they are ready to mate. Once pandas mate, they separate and the females raise the young alone.
- A newborn panda is only about the size of a hamster and weighs about 3½ ounces (100 g). Pandas are born without teeth and with their eyes closed. And they have only a thin covering of hair. It takes a few weeks for the typical black-and-white markings to appear.
- Young pandas stay with their mothers for about a year and a half. They learn how to find food, climb trees, and stay away from enemies.
- Pandas drink a lot and the cool mountain streams provide lots of fresh water year round.
- Many years ago, much of China was covered with bamboo forests. But as China's human population grew, the forests were cleared to make room for villages and rice fields. The bamboo from the forests was used for building homes, heating homes, and cooking food.
- Over time, much of the pandas' mountain forests disappeared and their populations started to decline. Today, there are about 900 pandas left in the wild.
- People used to hunt pandas for their beautiful black-and-white fur. They used the panda's skin to make sleeping mats that were warm and soft. Some people believed the mats kept evil spirits away from their homes.
- The government of China is doing many things to help save the panda. For one thing, people are no longer allowed to hunt pandas, and stiff penalties are enforced. The government has also established 12 special panda parks, or reserves, in China and is giving the pandas extra food during winters when there isn't enough bamboo.
- Scientists in China and around the world are working together to study pandas in the wild to learn more about how they live. These scientists are also trying to breed pandas in zoos so that the young can be released into the wild. Today there are about 80 giant pandas living in captivity in China and about 20 pandas at zoos in other parts of the world. The National Zoo in Washington, DC has two pandas, which were gifts from the Chinese government.

Habitat Is Home

In this two-part activity your kids will discover what habitats are, why they are so important to wildlife, and some of the ways endangered plants' and animals' habitats are being changed.

PART 1: HABITAT PICTURES

Begin by introducing the term *habitat* to the kids. Explain that the places where plants and animals live are called their homes, or habitats. Show the kids some pictures of deserts, prairies, oceans, and other habitats. Then tell them that within their habitats, plants and animals find everything they need to survive.

Next ask the kids what animals and plants need to survive. List their answers on a chalkboard or sheet of easel paper. They should be able to conclude that all living things need food, water, space, and shelter, as well sunlight, air, and other physical features.

Now pass out drawing paper and crayons or markers, and have the kids draw a habitat scene featuring a forest, meadow, or other type of habitat in your area. Explain that they should draw some of the plants and animals that live in the habitat, as well as some of the important things the plants and animals get from the habitat. For example, they could draw a forest scene showing trees and other plants, forest animals, a stream, the sun, soil, and other forest features. Afterward discuss their pictures.

PART 2: DISAPPEARING HOMES

Begin this part of the activity by explaining what *endangered* means. Show the kids pictures of endangered species, such as giant pandas, Kemp's ridley sea turtles, whooping cranes, and green pitcher plants. Next ask the kids why they think these plants and animals are in trouble. Explain that some plants and animals are in trouble because of over-collecting, unregulated hunting, or because people have introduced other kinds of animals or plants into their habitats. (For more about these problems see pages 34-36.)

Now tell the kids that the main reason most of these species are disappearing is that their habitats are being changed by people. Then pass out a copy of page 31 and three different colored markers or crayons to each child. Tell the kids that each of the large pictures in the middle of the page represents a way people are changing plant and animal habitats. And the smaller pictures at the top and bottom of the page depict some of the reasons why people change habitats. (You might want to quickly go over these smaller pictures so that the kids understand what they represent.)

Have the kids look at picture 1. Ask them what's happening in the picture. (People are filling in a wetland.) Can they find any of the smaller pictures that show a reason why people might fill or drain wetlands? (for space to build *buildings* and *roads,* and to create *farms* [to grow *food*] and *pasture*) As you go over each of the reasons, have the kids draw a line from picture 1 to the smaller picture. (They should use the same color marker or crayon for each line. See diagram.)

Next have the kids look at picture 2 and describe what's happening. Explain that many plants and animals lose their homes when people cut down forests. Ask them which of the smaller pictures show reasons why people cut down forests. (for *lumber, furniture,* and *firewood*; to clear areas for *buildings, roads,* and *dams*; to clear land for *farms* to grow *food*; to clear land for *pastures* so domestic animals such as cows and sheep can graze) Have the kids use a different colored marker to connect picture 2 to the smaller pictures.

Finally have the kids look at picture 3. Tell them that when people let too many cows, sheep, and other domestic animals graze in an area for a long time, the area may become *overgrazed:* So many of the plants may be eaten or trampled that the ground loses its protective plant cover and the soil washes away. Livestock may also compact the soil so much that native plants can't grow back. And sometimes there aren't enough plants left for wildlife to eat. Which of the small pictures shows products we get from grazing animals? (*food* [meat, milk] and *leather, wool,* and other products) Have the kids use the third

marker to connect picture 3 to the small pictures.

After your discussion ask the kids if they can think of any other ways people can change habitats. (mining operations, driving off-road vehicles or walking off designated trails, polluting, dredging marshes, and so on) Point out that people need to grow food, build houses, etc., but that sometimes we make too many changes in an area and create a lot of problems for the plants and animals that live there. Then pass out copies of page 16 and tell the kids that all of the species on the page are endangered or threatened, and that one of the main reasons they are in trouble is that people are changing their habitats. Finally, let the kids color the picture page and the habitat page.

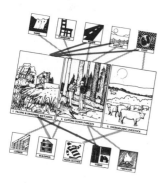
finished Copycat Page

All Around the World

Match animals and plants to where they live on a world map, then design a button or headband.

Objectives:
Define endangered and threatened. Describe the habitats of several endangered or threatened species. Explain that most species are in trouble due to habitat loss.

Ages:
Intermediate

Materials:
- *copies of pages 16 and 17*
- *copies of the map on page 26*
- *reference books*
- *thin cardboard*
- *drawing paper*
- *scissors*
- *glue*
- *crayons or markers*
- *tape*
- *safety pins*

Subjects:
Science and Geography

By focusing on 25 endangered and threatened species from around the world, your kids will see that a variety of plants and animals are in danger of becoming extinct. They will also discover that habitat loss is either directly or indirectly responsible for most of these species' problems.

brown hyena

PART 1: WHERE IN THE WORLD?

Begin by passing out copies of pages 16 and 17 to each child. Tell the kids that each of the plants and animals pictured on the pages is either endangered or threatened. Read through the names of the plants and animals with the kids so that they know how to pronounce each one.

Next divide the kids into several teams and pass out a copy of the map on page 26 to each child. Explain that each of the numbered areas on the map is home to one of the animals or plants on the Copycat Pages. The kids must research each plant and animal to find a number on the map within its range. Point out that the entire range of each species is not shown. For example, jaguars are found from Mexico to Brazil and humpback whales

are found in many parts of the world's oceans. Also point out that because some of the species' ranges overlap, one number might have more than one answer. For example, 9 and 11 could be noonday snails or green pitcher plants. Even though a few of the species are interchangeable, most can be figured out by the process of elimination. For example, the jaguar could be 5, 6, or 7. But because the quetzal can be only 5 and the vicuña can be only 7, the jaguar must be 5.

Then tell the kids that as they do their research, they must find out what kind of habitat (or habitats) each plant or animal lives in. Also have them jot down any interesting facts that they discover about each plant or animal and any information

25

they find about why each one is in trouble.

Encourage the kids to divide the work among their team members. Also remind them to try to focus their research on the specific animal or plant in each picture. For example, they should research *Philippine eagles,* not *eagles.* (*Note:* The kids may have trouble finding out anything about the plants, the Queen Alexandra birdwing butterfly, and the noonday snail. To make things easier you can pass out the information under "What's What" about these specific plants and animals. If you're working with younger kids you might want to divide the plants and animals among the entire group so that each child is responsible for only one.)

When the kids are finished, use the information under "What's What" to go over the map and discuss the animals and plants, the kinds of habitats they live in, and why they are in trouble. (The answers to the map are in parentheses at the end of each blurb.) After you've finished talking about all of the plants and animals, point out that most of these species are in trouble because of habitat loss. Explain that even though other problems, such as unregulated hunting, overcollecting, and pollution are very serious, habitat loss is by far the most pressing problem for wildlife species around the world.

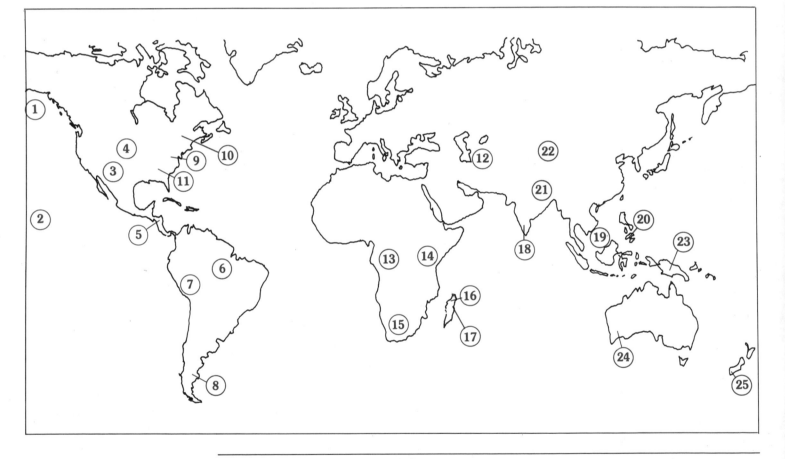

PART 2: PINS AND HEADBANDS

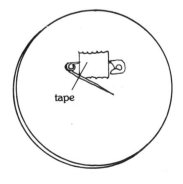

back of pin

tape

Now that the kids are familiar with some of the plants and animals that are threatened and endangered, where they live, and why they are in trouble, have them let other people know more about these species by making a button or headband. Pass out strips of drawing

DUGONGS NEED YOUR HELP

26

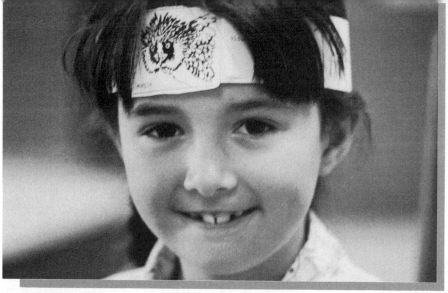
Luise Woelflein

paper (approximately 2 inches [5 cm] wide and 24 inches [60 cm] long) for the headbands and pieces of thin cardboard, safety pins, and tape for the buttons. Explain that to make their buttons and headbands, they can cut apart and use the plant and animal pictures on their Copycat Pages. Also explain that each button or headband should have a catchy slogan and must show the animal or plant in its habitat.

WHAT'S WHAT

Aye-aye (EYE-eye)—endangered; lives in the tropical rain forests of Madagascar; eats fruit and insect larvae; is a primate; in trouble mainly due to habitat loss (16 or 17)

Queen Alexandra birdwing butterfly—listed on CITES II (see page 65); lives in the tropical rain forests of Papua New Guinea; largest butterfly in the world; in trouble mainly due to habitat loss (23)

Brady's pincushion cactus—endangered; lives in the desert in northern Arizona; gets up to 2 inches (5 cm) wide and 2 inches (5 cm) high; shrivels up during the hottest months of the year; in trouble mainly due to habitat loss and overcollecting (3)

Dugong—endangered; lives in coastal shallows of Indian and southwestern Pacific Oceans; feeds on sea grasses; may be 10 feet (3 m) long; in trouble due to unregulated hunting (19)

Philippine eagle—endangered; lives in tropical rain forests of the Philippine Islands; eats birds, reptiles, and small mammals; wingspan may be 7 feet (2 m); in trouble mainly due to habitat loss and unregulated hunting (20)

Black-footed ferret—endangered; lives in the western prairies of North America; eats mainly prairie dogs; in trouble mainly due to eating poisoned prairie dogs (4)

Gavial (GAY-vee-uhl)—endangered; lives in rivers in India, Nepal, Bangladesh, and Pakistan; eats fish; in trouble due to unregulated hunting and habitat disruption (18)

Brown hyena—endangered; lives in dry grassland, open scrub, and semidesert areas of southern Africa; feeds mainly on dead animals; in trouble due to unregulated hunting (15)

Indri (IN-dree)—endangered; lives in the tropical rain forests of Madagascar; eats fruit and leaves; is a primate; in trouble mainly due to habitat loss (17 or 16)

Jaguar—endangered; lives in many areas from Mexico to Argentina, including tropical rain forests, swamps, and grasslands; eats deer, peccaries, and rodents, as well as turtles, frogs, and fish; in trouble due to unregulated hunting and habitat loss (6)

Kakapo (KAH-kah poh)—endangered; lives in forests and grasslands of New Zealand; is a parrot; unable to fly, but can glide; eats fruit and nectar; in trouble mainly due to predation by introduced species (25)

Snow leopard—endangered; lives in the mountains of central Asia; eats mammals such as ibex, wild sheep, deer, and hares, as well as birds; in trouble mainly due to unregulated hunting (22)

Mandrill—endangered; lives in tropical rain forests of

western Africa; eats fruit, seeds, roots, insects, and fungi; adult males have brightly colored red and blue faces; in trouble mainly due to habitat loss (13)

Numbat—endangered; lives mainly in the eucalyptus forests in parts of Western Australia; eats mainly termites; is a marsupial; in trouble due to habitat loss and predation by introduced species (24)

Small whorled pogonia (orchid)—endangered; lives in open areas of hardwood forests from Ontario to northern Georgia; in trouble mainly due to habitat alteration (10)

Green pitcher plant—endangered; lives in wetlands in Alabama, Georgia, and Tennessee; digests insects; in trouble due to habitat alteration and overcollecting (11 or 9)

Resplendent quetzal (ket-SAHL)—endangered; lives in tropical rain forests of Central America; eats mainly fruit; male's tail feathers may be more than 2 feet (60 cm) long; in trouble due to habitat loss, unregulated hunting, and overcollecting for the pet trade (5)

Darwin's rhea—endangered; lives in grasslands in parts of Peru, Brazil, and Argentina; in trouble due to unregulated hunting and habitat loss (8)

Noonday snail—threatened; lives in forests in North Caro-

lina; in trouble due to habitat loss (9 or 11)

Loggerhead sea turtle—threatened; lives in tropical and temperate oceans; eats mainly bottom-dwelling mollusks and crustaceans; may weigh 300 pounds (135 kg); in trouble because of pollution, destruction of nesting beaches, and accidental capture in shrimp nets (2)

Urial—endangered; lives in parts of Asia; is a wild sheep; eats woody shrubs and grasses; in trouble due to unregulated hunting, predation by feral dogs, and habitat loss (12)

Vicuña (vi-KOON-yah)—endangered; lives in Andes Mountains in Peru, Bolivia, Chile, and Argentina; eats grasses; in trouble due to unregulated hunting (7)

Humpback whale—endangered; lives in oceans from poles to tropical waters; eats small, shrimplike animals and fish; may weigh over 30 tons (27 t); in trouble mainly due to unregulated hunting (1)

Wild yak—endangered; lives in mountains of central Asia; eats grasses, herbs, and lichens; may stand over 6½ feet (2 m) at the shoulder; in trouble due to unregulated hunting (21)

Grevy's zebra—threatened; lives in arid grasslands and on hillsides in parts of eastern Africa; eats grasses; in trouble mainly due to habitat loss and unregulated hunting (14)

Sizing Up Reserves

 If you wanted to create a tropical rain forest reserve in South America that was large enough to protect most of the species that live there, how big would the reserve have to be? No one really knows for sure, but scientists working in Brazil may have an answer sometime in the next few years. These scientists are in the midst of a 20-year study to find out what happens when parts of a rain forest are cut down and how the size of the remaining forest affects the plants and animals that live there. By looking at some of the data these scientists have collected so far, your kids will discover some of the ways tropical rain forest destruction affects certain species. And they'll also learn some of the ways species in a rain forest community interact and how much space it might take to preserve them.

Before you get started, copy the diagram in the margin onto a chalkboard or sheet of easel paper. Then begin by having the kids imagine that a road is going to be built right through the middle of a huge section of tropical rain forest. Also, some of the forested land is going to be converted into pastures for cattle and farmland for crops.

Ask the kids how life in the forest might be affected by these changes. (Some animals might be killed on the road; others might move into less developed areas; more development might come into the area because of the access the road provides, causing further destruction of the rain forest; entire species could become extinct [see the note on the next page].) List their answers on a chalkboard or sheet of easel paper.

After the kids have made some predictions, try the following demonstration to get them thinking about some of the other changes that can occur when parts of a forest are cut down. (This demonstration works best with a group of at least 20 kids.)

CHOPPING DOWN THE FOREST

Have the kids stand close together in a big group in an open area of the room. Tell them that each one of them is a tree, and together they represent a huge tract of undisturbed tropical rain forest. Have one child in the center of the forest describe

Luise Woelflein

what he or she sees when looking "through the trees." Can he or she see the forest edge? you? the rest of the room? Is there much light down near the floor? (Point out that, in many tropical rain forests, the canopy is so thick that little sunlight reaches the forest floor.) Then turn a small electric fan on low at the edge of the forest and ask the center child if he or she can feel a breeze.

Now "chop down" part of the forest by having some of the kids near the edge move aside. (Pick kids from each "side" of the edge.) Ask the center child to report any changes in what he or she can see. Turn the fan on low again, and ask if the center child can feel a breeze. Once part of the forest has been cut down, the center child should notice more light near the floor, should find it easier to see through the trees to the edge of the forest, and should be able to feel a much stronger breeze. If none of these changes occur, chop down some more of the trees at the edge.

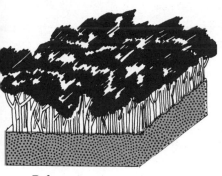

continuous forest

Before

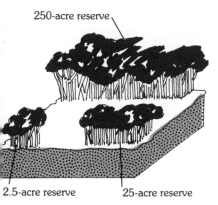

250-acre reserve

2.5-acre reserve   25-acre reserve

After

After the demonstration, ask the kids what has happened to the area that used to be the middle of the forest. (It's now at or near the forest's edge.) Then ask them how this shift from forest middle to forest edge might affect the life within the forest. Point out that many of the plants and animals that were adapted to living in the middle of the forest might not be able to survive at the forest edge. Can the kids think of reasons for this? (Changes in temperature, moisture level, air circulation, and so on would occur at the forest's new edge. For example, the former "middle of the forest" would now receive much more sunlight than before, raising the overall temperature of the area. The area would also receive more wind, which could make the new edge drier than when it was part of the forest's middle.) Again, list the kids' answers on the chalkboard or a piece of easel paper.

Now tell the kids that some scientists in Brazil are studying what happens to the life in a rain forest when part of the forest is cut down. Then, using the information under "What's Happening in Brazil?" on page 30, explain the Biological Dynamics of Forest Fragments Project. Make sure the kids understand that the forest in the area where the scientists are working was going to be cut down anyway. But by directing where the loggers cut, the scientists have been able to create reserves, or forest "islands," of specific sizes. Show the kids the diagram you copied earlier to give them a better idea of what it is these scientists are doing.

Also explain that the scientists are trying to figure out how big a reserve might have to be in order to protect as many of the species that live in a rain forest as possible. For example, could most of the plants and most of the birds, mammals, amphibians, and other animals found in the Brazilian rain forest survive in a 2500-acre (1000-ha) reserve or would it take a 25,000-acre (10,000-ha) reserve? Or one that's even larger? (*Note:* Explain that new research shows that some species are so specialized that they may become extinct if even a small area in certain parts of a rain forest is destroyed.)

Afterward pass out copies of page 32 so the kids can see some of the things that have happened in the isolated reserves in the Forest Fragments project. Explain that the charts and graphs show real data that the scientists have collected from 2.5-acre (1-ha) and 25-acre (10-ha) reserves during the reserves' first two years of isolation. Then pass out copies of page 33 and have the kids answer the questions using the charts and graphs.

When the kids are finished, ask them if any of the changes they predicted earlier occurred in the reserves the scientists studied. Talk about the changes, then go over the answers to the questions (see the end of this activity). As you go over the answers, discuss the fact that all animals and plants depend on specific physical conditions in their habitats in order to survive. For example, when light conditions changed in the forest areas the scientists were studying, many of the butterfly species that had lived in the forest's interior disappeared. And trees that were once in the interior were damaged and even knocked over by increased wind.

Also point out that all animals and plants depend on other species in order to survive and reproduce. For example, monkeys that eat fruit were absent or very rare in the reserves because many of the fruit trees they depended on had been cut down. (There were still some fruit trees left, but not enough to support the monkeys year round.)

You might also want to explain that all animals need a certain amount of space in order to find all the food and water they need to survive. For example, herds of white-lipped peccaries need thousands of acres. (For more about how much space certain animals need, see "A Home in a Range" on pages 43-45 of *NatureScope: Amazing Mammals—Part 1.*)

Finally, ask the kids if they think either a 2.5- or 25-acre (1- or 10-ha) reserve would be large enough to preserve the variety of life found in the Brazilian rain forest the scientists are studying. Tell them that even though the Forest Fragments project is far from over, scientists are predicting that a Brazilian rain forest reserve would probably have to cover millions of acres in order to protect most of the species that live there.

(continued next page)

WHAT'S HAPPENING IN BRAZIL?

In 1977, Dr. Thomas Lovejoy of World Wildlife Fund (WWF) was looking for a place to try an experiment. He wanted to find out what happens when parts of a tropical rain forest are separated by roads, pastures, and other human developments. He also wanted to try to find out how much forest it might take to make a reserve large enough to support the plants and animals that normally live in a rain forest.

Lovejoy knew that, under Brazilian law, any land development project in the Amazon region of Brazil must leave half of the area forested. He discovered some land that was going to be converted to pasture and asked if he could direct which parts of the total area would be converted to pasture and which ones would be left undisturbed. The local government, Brazilian scientists, and the ranchers agreed to cooperate.

In 1979, scientists from WWF and Brazil's National Institute for Amazon Research began mapping out more than 20 areas within the virgin rain forest. These areas would eventually become reserves of varying sizes: 2.5, 25, 250, and 2500 acres (1, 10, 100, 1000 ha). There was also one 25,000-acre (10,000-ha) reserve. Then, with help from more scientists and some of the ranchers, they obtained a "before" picture of each future reserve by taking an inventory of the plants and animals in each one.

Finally, in 1980, the ranchers started cutting down the forest. The reserves, once part of a continuous forest, became isolated "islands" of trees. And the scientists immediately started monitoring the changes that occurred in each "island." So far only 10 of the reserves have been *isolated,* or separated from the continuous forest. The scientists are planning to continue the experiment until at least 1999.

BRANCHING OUT: MEASURE THE DIFFERENCE

Temperature variation between the edge of a forest and its interior occurs in all forests—not just in tropical rain forests. To help your kids see how temperatures vary between the inside and outside of a forest, take them to a nearby woodlot and have them measure the temperature at the edge of the woods, just inside the woods, and 50 feet (15 m) or more into the woods.

You can also measure differences in evaporation rate and soil moisture. To get an idea of differences in evaporation rate, hang one wet cloth inside the forest and one outside and see how long it takes each to dry. And to determine soil moisture differences you can just feel the soil both inside and outside the forest. (In general, soil in a forest holds more moisture than that outside a forest.) After taking your measurements, discuss the fact that many of the animals and plants that are adapted to conditions within a forest often can't survive outside a forest—or even at its edge.

Note: The Biological Dynamics of Forest Fragments Project used to be called the Minimum Critical Size of Ecosystems Project. The name was changed to better reflect the expanded scope of the project.

Answers to Copycat Page Questions:

1. ***a.*** When part of the forest was cut down, the birds that lived there crowded into the reserves, and at first more birds were caught per net per hour. However, because the reserves didn't have enough space and food for all the birds, many of them died or left and the number of birds caught per net per hour soon dropped. In comparison, the number of birds caught per net per hour in the continuous forest stayed about the same before and after the reserves were isolated.

2. ***c.*** Many of the original butterfly species disappeared from the reserves after the reserves were isolated, and others survived only in the centers of the larger reserves. The increase in the total number of butterfly species present in the reserves was the result of light-loving butterfly species moving into the light-filled edges of the reserves.

3. ***b.*** The reserves were too small for most of the mammals shown in Table 1. In fact, of all the primates, only red howler monkeys were able to survive in large numbers in the larger reserves. (Unlike most of these other primates, which eat mainly fruit, red howler monkeys eat leaves. When the reserves were isolated many of the fruit trees were chopped down. But the red howler monkeys could still find plenty of leaves to eat.)

4. ***In the reserves.*** The number of standing dead trees and the number of trees uprooted or broken by wind or the fall of another tree were all higher in the reserves than in the continuous forest. And the numbers jumped within two years. For example, the number of standing dead trees in one 25-acre reserve was 9 the first year and 65 the second year.

5. The reserves were too small for the white-lipped peccaries so they disappeared. When the peccaries disappeared from the reserves their wallows slowly dried up. And once the wallows were gone the frogs had no puddles to lay their eggs in and so they disappeared too.

DAMS

FURNITURE

ROADS

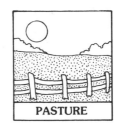

PASTURE

FOOD

1. FILLING & DRAINING WETLANDS

2. CUTTING DOWN FORESTS

3. OVERGRAZING LIVESTOCK

LUMBER

BUILDINGS

WOOL/LEATHER

FARMS

FIREWOOD

GRAPH 1

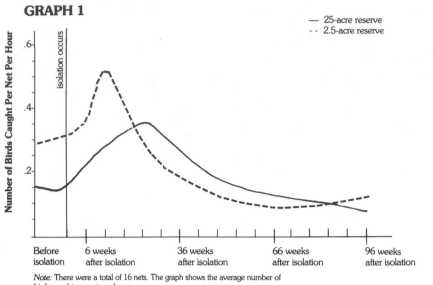

— 25-acre reserve
-- 2.5-acre reserve

Note: There were a total of 16 nets. The graph shows the average number of birds caught per net per hour.

GRAPH 2

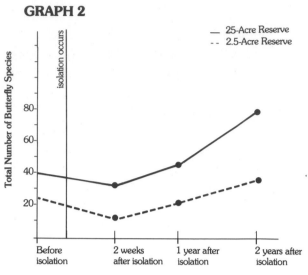

— 25-Acre Reserve
-- 2.5-Acre Reserve

TABLE 1

Mammal	Continuous Forest	25–Acre Reserve	2.5–Acre Reserve
Red howler monkey	very abundant	very abundant	absent
White-faced saki (monkey)	rare	absent	absent
Golden-handed tamarin (monkey)	abundant	absent	absent
Collared peccary (pig like mammal)	abundant	absent	absent
Acouchi (large rodent)	very abundant	rare	absent
Paca (large rodent)	abundant	absent	absent
Rice rat	rare	rare	rare
Nine-banded armadillo	very abundant	rare	absent

TABLE 2

Death Rates of Trees 2 Years After Isolation	
2.5-acre reserve	2.6%
25-acre reserve	2.6%
continuous forest	1.5%

The 2.5- and 25-acre reserves were hotter and drier than the continuous forest. And temperatures between the edges and 300 feet within one 250-acre reserve varied by as much as 8° F.

1. **Which of the following statements best describes what happened to the *number of birds caught per net per hour* in the reserves?**
   a. The number nearly doubled just after the reserves were isolated and then dropped dramatically. After 96 weeks the number was lower than before the reserves were isolated.
   b. The number slowly increased in the reserves after the reserves were isolated and kept increasing for 96 weeks.
   c. The number remained unchanged.

2. **Which of the following statements best describes the second graph?**
   a. The number of butterfly species decreased steadily for two years after the reserves were isolated.
   b. Immediately after the reserves were isolated, the number of butterfly species dropped. But after two years the number was the same as before isolation.
   c. Immediately after the reserves were isolated, the number of butterfly species dropped. But after two years there were more kinds of butterflies than before isolation.

3. **Which of the following statements best describes the information in Table 1?**
   a. Most of the mammals present in the continuous forest were just as common in the reserves.
   b. Most of the mammals present in the continuous forest were absent from the reserves.
   c. Most of the mammals were rare in both the reserves and the continuous forest.

4. **Look at the information in Table 2. Did a greater percentage of trees die in the reserves or in the continuous forest?**

5. **After three years, no barred leaf frogs were found within the 25- or 2.5-acre reserves. Several other kinds of leaf frogs had disappeared as well, even though other kinds of frogs were still found in the reserves. Given the following information, why do you think the barred leaf frogs disappeared?**
   - Barred leaf frogs lay their eggs in puddles.
   - White-lipped peccaries are piglike mammals that live in herds. These herds need thousands of acres of undisturbed forest in order to find all the food they need to survive.
   - When white-lipped peccaries wallow in the mud they create small puddles.

POACHERS, POISONS, & OTHER PROBLEMS

F or three days, special agents had tailed the two men from the pick-up site in New Orleans. Now, near a warehouse in New Jersey, the chase was over. One agent, disguised as a back-alley derelict, watched as four men joined the original two and began unloading several bags from the car. On his signal, the other agents moved in and arrested the smugglers for illegal possession and transportation of 509 alligator hides.

This is just one example of the dozens of arrests that the U.S. Fish and Wildlife Service makes each year to try to stop the illegal trade of rare and endangered wildlife. But even the most determined efforts by law enforcement officials won't stop smuggling as long as people keep buying crocodile shoes, snakeskin belts, exotic birds, and other wildlife products and pets. The illegal plant and animal trade—both of products and of live plants and animals—is just one of the ways that people are directly and indirectly endangering plants and animals around the world.

TAKING TOO MANY

Although it is illegal in most countries to kill rare and endangered plants and animals and sell them or products made from them, many people throughout the world still do it. And although it is illegal to possess rare and endangered plants and animals or products made from them, many people still buy them. Here's a look at some of these illegal activities:

Tricks of the Trade: Daggers made from rhino horns, jewelry fashioned from sea turtle shells, and fur coats made from jaguar skins are just a few of the wildlife products illegally sold each year. In addition to these products, many endangered plants are sold as houseplants and many endangered animals are sold as pets. Trade in live animals and plants and the products made from them is the second greatest factor endangering species. (Habitat destruction is the first. For more about this problem, see pages 19-21.) The demand for these products is so great that once-plentiful species are becoming rare, and already-rare species have reached critically low numbers. Despite laws passed to protect species in trouble, potential profits (Asian rhino horns can sell for several thousand dollars a pound) make poaching worth the risk to some people. (For more about laws protecting threatened and endangered species, see page 65.)

Private Collectors: Ironically, some of the greatest admirers of rare species are pushing them closer to extinction. Butterfly, snake, and cactus collectors, for example, often buy and collect rare specimens to add to their private collections. In doing this, they are often depleting already threatened populations for their own enjoyment. And many of these collectors support the illegal trade of animals and plants since they will pay dealers large sums of money for rare species.

Illegal Harvest: Another threat to wildlife—especially to large game animals—is illegal or poorly regulated trophy hunting. Trophy hunting reached its peak of popularity in the late 19th century when big game hunters could legally kill tigers, cheetahs, zebras, oryxes, and other animals. But in spite of laws passed to protect these and other animals, illegal trophy hunting of endangered animals continues.

Cutting Out the Competition: About 70 years ago, the Biological Survey of the United States, which was the forerunner of the Fish and Wildlife Service, paid trappers and hunters to kill predators such as wolves, bobcats, lynx, and cougars.

At that time, people believed these and other predators killed significant numbers of livestock, fish, and game, thereby reducing the harvest for people. This prejudice against predators continues today, even though we now know that in general, predators don't significantly reduce the populations of fish, domestic livestock, or game animals.

Note: Some species of ducks, geese, rabbits, pheasants, deer, and other animals, which are abundant in many parts of the world, can be legally hunted or trapped at certain times of the year. This harvest is regulated so that populations of each species do not become depleted. However, illegal trapping and hunting, or *poaching,* can sometimes endanger wildlife populations—especially if a species is already rare. Poaching includes unlawful trophy hunting, illegal market hunting, and violations of hunting restrictions, such as taking more animals than the legal limit allows or hunting out of season.

EXOTICS, POISONS, AND POLLUTION

It's easy to see that plant and animal populations can be wiped out if too many individuals are illegally killed for their fur, meat, or other products, or are collected and sold in pet or plant stores. But many species around the world are in danger of becoming extinct for reasons that aren't so obvious. Here's a look at some of the ways people are unintentionally endangering wildlife species:

Uninvited Guests: Introducing non-native, or *exotic,* species to an area can present a lot of problems for the animals and plants already living there—especially for those species that are already rare. That's because all newcomers compete with the native plants and animals for food, water, shelter, and space. Most introduced plants and animals are not problems in their native lands. It's only when they are introduced into areas where they have no natural enemies that they start to cause trouble. (For more about the problems associated with introduced species, see "Paradise Lost" on page 39.)

Poisons: When people use herbicides and pesticides to get rid of "pest" species, the poisons often harm more than just the pests. These potent chemicals can accidentally kill many non-pest plants and animals, including certain mammals, insects, fish, and birds. In many cases the poisons can stay potent for hundreds of years and can slowly build up to toxic levels in the tissues of plants and animals. For example, before DDT was banned in the U.S., high levels of the pesticide were found in brown pelicans, falcons, bald eagles, and many other birds. The DDT caused eggshell thinning, and many birds were crushed before they hatched.

Acid from the Sky: Acid rain is a problem that many scientists think is seriously endangering trees, fish, aquatic plants, insects, and many other types of plants and animals around the world. (Acid rain occurs when sulfur and nitrogen compounds in the atmosphere react with water vapor and fall as acidic rain.)

Wicked Waters: Water pollution is a major threat to species worldwide. Here's a look at some of the ways water pollution is harming wildlife:

- Raw sewage and toxic chemicals are continually dumped into many lakes, rivers, and streams, poisoning birds, fish, plants, and other forms of life. Although state, local, and federal efforts to help clean up polluted waterways are

immature brown pelican

Leonard Lee Rue III

continuing, the problem is still extremely serious. For example, experts estimate that the water in one-fourth of the national wildlife refuges in the United States has been poisoned by toxic substances.

- Oil spills in both freshwater and marine environments have threatened entire populations of fish and aquatic birds and mammals.
- Plastic waste (bags, strapping, six-pack rings, and so on) floating in oceans can kill sea mammals, birds, and turtles. The animals may mistake the plastic for food and starve with a stomach full of indigestible material or a beak wrapped shut in plastic.
- Plastic nets lost by fishermen have been left to float in ocean waters for years. These ghost nets "fish" as they float, capturing seals, dolphins, turtles, sea birds, and other sea creatures, and eventually causing them to drown.
- Lead shotgun pellets at the bottoms of marshes and ponds are accidentally eaten by waterfowl. The lead builds up in the birds' bodies, poisoning them and any other animals that might feed on them.

In the Wrong Place at the Wrong Time: Automobiles, boats, and other vehicles have unintentionally taken a toll on wildlife. For example, scientists estimate that at least one Florida panther is killed by a car each year. Considering that the number of Florida panthers in the wild is probably fewer than 50, traffic deaths represent a major threat to these endangered cats. Another problem occurs in open waterways where motorboat propellers inflict wounds on endangered manatees. Sometimes these wounds can be fatal.

THE PROBLEMS ADD UP

Most plants and animals are not in trouble because of just one problem. Most are threatened or endangered due to a combination of factors. Atlantic salmon, for instance, are in trouble because they are overfished, are sensitive to water pollution and the effects of acid rain, and can't make their annual migration upstream because dams block their way. And bald eagles suffer from "predator persecution," loss of habitat, and poisoning from lead shot and pesticides.

Despite the complexities of the problems facing many vanishing species, there have been many success stories. See the background information on pages 50-51 for more about how people are helping some species make a comeback.

Wheel of Trouble

Make a wheel that shows why some sea turtles are endangered.

Objective:
Explain why some sea turtles are endangered.

Ages:
Primary

Materials:
- *pictures of sea turtles*
- *pictures of land-dwelling turtles (optional)*
- *copies of page 45*
- *crayons or markers*
- *lightweight paper plates at least 9" (23 cm) in diameter*
- *scissors*
- *glue*
- *tape*
- *construction paper (optional)*
- *paper fasteners*

Subject:
Science

finished wheel

attach construction paper legs, head, and tail

any sea turtles are endangered for a lot of the same reasons that other species are in trouble, including overcollecting, habitat loss, and pollution. By using sea turtles as an example, younger children can learn about the variety of problems that affect many endangered species.

Before you begin, make eight triangular patterns, following the directions under "Getting Ready" below. Then start the activity by showing the kids pictures of sea turtles and talking about their natural history. (For general information about sea turtles, see "Turtle Talk" on the next page.)

Now tell the kids that most sea turtles are endangered or threatened. Explain to the kids that they will be learning why these animals are in trouble by making a special "wheel of trouble." Then give each child a copy of page 45, two paper plates, scissors, glue, a paper fastener, and crayons or markers. Also hand out the triangular patterns you made earlier and tell the kids to share them. Then have them follow the directions at the bottom of the page to make a "wheel of trouble."

GETTING READY

1. Cut out the circle on page 45 and tape it to the back of a paper plate. (Don't use too much tape because you will eventually be removing the circle.)
2. Cut out each segment, making sure you don't cut through the center circle or cut along the outer edge (see diagram). After cutting out each pattern, remove the paper pieces. (You will end up with four separate segments.)
3. Repeat this with another plate and Copycat Page. (Or use the pattern pieces to cut out four more segments from another plate.) Eight pattern pieces should be enough to get a group of 25 started.

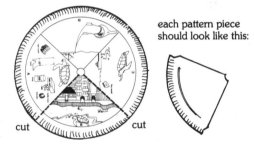

each pattern piece should look like this:

HOW TO MAKE THE WHEEL OF TROUBLE

1. Color the pictures on the Copycat Page, then cut out the circle along the solid outer line.
2. Glue the circle on the back of a paper plate. (Tell the kids to use a *thin* layer of glue.) Set this plate aside.
3. Lay the triangular pattern on the back of the other paper plate so that the edge of the pattern meets the edge of the plate. Trace it and cut out the shape. (When one child finishes using a pattern piece, he or she can pass it on to someone else.)
4. Place the cut-out plate on top of the plate with the pictures and push a paper fastener through the center of both plates. (If you're using thick paper plates, you may have to first poke a hole through the plates with scissors or a pen.)

As the kids turn the top or bottom plate, each of the four pictures will appear in the cut-out space. Explain that these pictures illustrate the four major problems sea turtles face. Have the kids turn their wheels to picture A, then use the information under "Trouble for Turtles" to talk about each of the problems.

After your discussion, have the kids draw a picture of a sea turtle on their top plate and write the title "Why Sea Turtles Are in Trouble." You can also have the kids cut legs, a head, and a tail out of construction paper, and tape them to the bottom plate to make the wheel look like a turtle (see diagram). *(continued next page)*

TROUBLE FOR TURTLES

A. *Meat, shells, skin, and eggs:* Overharvesting is a major problem for sea turtles. They are killed for their beautiful shells (which are made into jewelry), for their skin (which is tanned and used to make boots, belts, shoes, and bags), and for food (people eat their meat and eggs and use the cartilage to make soup).

B. *Changing beaches:* Development is another problem for sea turtles. In many areas, people have built homes, roads, motels, and other types of development on the beaches where sea turtles nest. Turtles don't usually lay their eggs in these built-up areas, but if they do, the hatchlings have problems. Most turtles hatch at night and instinctively head for the ocean. Many scientists think the hatchlings may be guided by the brightness of the sky over the water. But on developed beaches, the newly hatched turtles may be mistakenly guided to the bright lights of buildings. These hatchlings often dry up in the sun the next day or get eaten by predators.

C. *Pollution:* When plastic garbage is dumped into the oceans, it can cause big problems for many sea turtles. That's because turtles may mistake floating plastic bags for jellyfish and swallow them. They can't digest the plastic, and if it blocks a turtle's esophagus, the animal will slowly starve.

Other forms of pollution, such as oil, tar, and poisonous chemicals released into the oceans, are also dangerous, especially for young turtles.

D. *Fishing nets:* Every year, some sea turtles drown when they are accidentally caught in shrimp nets. To help solve this problem, some shrimpers are now using Turtle Excluder Devices (TEDs) that fit inside shrimp nets and release the trapped turtles.

Note: The five sea turtles listed below are all affected by these four problems. But some problems are more severe for certain species. For example, hawksbill turtles are overhunted for their shells and eggs. But because they live in areas where shrimp fishing is not a big business, they are rarely caught in fishing nets. For simplicity, we didn't include which problems affect each species.

TURTLE TALK

The Kemp's ridley, Pacific ridley, loggerhead, green, and hawksbill sea turtles are all threatened or endangered. The following facts apply generally to these five turtles:

- live in warm oceans around the world
- eat jellyfish, sponges, crabs, fish, and/or plants, depending on the species
- size can range from 3 to 4 feet (.9–1.2 m) and weight can range from 100 to 350 pounds (45–158 kg)
- may live as many as 70 years
- have paddle-shaped flippers that help them move through the water and streamlined shells that reduce water resistance (compare to pictures of land turtles with high-domed shells and clawed feet)
- lay their eggs on sandy beaches; use their back flippers to dig deep holes in the sand, where they lay up to 100 eggs
- eggs hatch in about two months
- many young turtles are eaten by birds, crabs, fish, and other predators
- adult turtles have only two enemies—sharks and people

For more information about how sea turtles lay their eggs, read this story to your group: *Look Out for Loggerheads* by Pat Hughey (*Ranger Rick*, July 1983, pp 4-7).

hawksbill sea turtle

Paradise Lost

Take part in a short play and then take a walk to find introduced species.

Objectives:
Describe how introduced species can affect native plants and animals. Name some introduced species in your area.

Ages:
Primary and Intermediate

Materials:
- *open area*
- *colored crepe paper streamers*
- *plastic pantyhose eggs*
- *world map*
- *markers or crayons*
- *pictures of native Hawaiian plants and birds (optional)*
- *scissors*
- *cardboard*
- *record or tape player and recording of waves on a beach (optional)*
- *materials for making costumes (optional)*
- *yardsticks (optional)*
- *butcher paper (optional)*

Subjects:
Science and Drama

 y putting on a short play about the loss of wildlife on the Hawaiian Islands, your kids can find out about the ways introduced species affect native plants and animals. Then they can search for introduced species in their own area.

Begin by pointing out Hawaii on a world map. Explain that many different kinds of plants and animals live on these islands, and that many of these species are found nowhere else in the world. Also mention that many more types of plants and animals once lived on Hawaii, but they have become extinct in the last 1500 years.

Explain that Hawaii first lost some of its native plants and animals after the Polynesians came to the islands, about 1500 years ago. (Point out Polynesia on the map.) The Polynesians brought along animals from their homelands that were very different from the creatures on Hawaii. These *introduced species* created serious problems for the native Hawaiian plants and animals, and many of the native species became extinct.

Then, over a thousand years later, explorers from Europe (point out Europe on the map) came to the islands and introduced even more new species to the islands. And even more native Hawaiian plants and animals died out.

Also point out that this type of problem is common on many islands, not just Hawaii. Then tell the kids they'll be putting on a short play to show just what happened.

PUTTING ON THE PLAY

First write the name of each character (see "Cast of Characters" below) on a separate slip of paper, put the slips in a sack, and have each person pick one. Adjust the number of roles to fit the size of your group. (You can play the part of the narrator or split it up among a few of the kids.)

Next have the players go over the movements and sounds that accompany each part. Tell them that whenever they hear their characters mentioned in the narration, they should make their assigned movements or sounds.

For props you can use plastic pantyhose eggs to represent bird eggs and simple cardboard cutouts to represent nests and food. You might also want to make a boat prop by cutting out a simple boat shape from cardboard or butcher paper (about 10 feet [3 m] long and 3 feet [1 m] tall) and reinforcing it with a yardstick at each end.

You can also have the kids make simple costumes (see suggestions below). And you can show them pictures of native Hawaiian plants and birds to help some of the kids design their own costumes.

CAST OF CHARACTERS

birds (native) **(5)** *movement*—hold arms near body and "flap"; *costume*—make shoulder sashes out of bright red streamers
Polynesians (2) *movement*—shield eyes with hand as if looking into distance; *costume*—flower garlands or garlands made from streamers
Europeans (2) *movement*—same as Polynesians; *costume*—make a simple explorer hat out of folded newspaper
pigs (4) *movement* and *sound*—stomp and "oink"; *costume*—make signs with small pictures of pigs
chickens (2) *movement* and *sound*—make scratching motions with feet, fold arms and hold them as wings, and "cluck"; *costume*—make signs with small pictures
cattle and goats (2) *movement* and *sounds*—stomp, "moo," and "baa"; *costume*—make signs with small pictures
plants (5) *movement*—hold arms over head and sway back and forth; *costume*—make shoulder sashes out of green streamers

rats (4) *movement*—make gnawing motions with teeth and crawl on hands and feet; *costume*—draw whiskers on the face with face paint
cats (2) *movement* and *sound*—hold fingers in the shape of claws, "meow"; *costume*—make ears and tail out of construction paper
non-native birds (2) *movement*—flap like native birds; *costume*—make shoulder sashes out of brown or blue streamers

INVADERS IN PARADISE

Setting the Scene: Find a large area inside or outside where the play can take place. Create an island by outlining an area about 20 feet (6 m) in diameter with green streamers. Hawaiian plants and birds should stand inside the island. Plastic pantyhose eggs (representing bird eggs) and cardboard food symbols (representing bird nests and food) should be scattered among the plants.

All introduced species and the explorers should stand behind the boat. As their characters are introduced, they should step over the streamers onto the island. For realism, you might want to softly play a tape of waves crashing on a beach.

Narrator: A long, long time ago, many kinds of animals and plants lived on the islands of Hawaii, including **birds** of all sizes and colors. Some **birds** ate fruit, others sipped nectar, and some fed on insects or seeds. And some made their nests on the ground, while others nested in the trees, bushes, and other **plants** on the islands.

Many of these Hawaiian **plants** were found nowhere else in the world. And unlike plants from other parts of the world, they had few defenses, such as spines, thorns, or poisonous chemicals in their leaves, to protect them from large grazing animals. They hadn't needed any protection because no large grazing animals had ever lived on the islands.

Then, about 1500 years ago, **Polynesians** from faraway islands sailed to the Hawaiian Islands. (Polynesians walk onto the island and stand near the edge of the island.) The **Polynesians** brought **pigs**, **chickens**, and other animals from their homelands. Some of these "new" animals escaped and began to roam wild in the forests. (Two pigs and both chickens enter island and walk into "forest.")

The **Polynesians** had accidentally brought other animals to the islands,

too, such as **rats**. These **rats** had been living on the boats and escaped onto the islands. (Two rats go into forest.)

All of these new animals caused problems for the **birds** and **plants** of Hawaii. The **rats** ate the birds' eggs. They could even climb trees to get the eggs. (Rats carry off eggs near trees.) The **chickens** ate some of the same foods that some native Hawaiian **birds** ate, leaving less food for the native **birds**. (Have the chickens carry off food symbols.)

And the **pigs** ate any birds' eggs they could find on the ground. (Pigs pick up some eggs.) They also ate many of the native **plants**.

The number of **chickens**, **pigs**, and **rats** kept growing and growing, and they kept eating more and more of the native birds' eggs and the native **plants**. Soon, many of these **plants** and **birds** became extinct. (Some of plants and birds sit down.)

But more trouble was still to come. Many years later, **Europeans** landed on the islands. (Europeans step onto the island.) They brought along **cattle**, **goats**, **cats**, and more **rats** and **pigs**! (Rest of animals follow.) And what do you think happened? The **cattle**, **goats**, and **pigs** ate many of the remaining native **plants**. (More plants sit down.) And the **rats** ate more **birds'** eggs and even full-grown **birds**! (Rats pick up more plastic eggs.) The **cats** also killed some of the **birds**. (Some native birds sit down.)

These **explorers** also brought **non-native birds** that carried diseases that made the native **birds** very sick. (Non-native birds come onto island.) Some of the native **birds** even died. (Another native bird sits down.)

As time went on, some more of the native **birds** became extinct, and more of the native **plants** also died out. (Most of remaining plants and birds sit down.) The islands of Hawaii had changed forever.

THE END

native Hawaiian honeycreeper

AFTER THE PLAY

Ask each group of characters to explain how their introduced species affected the native Hawaiian plants and animals. Then explain that no one will ever be exactly

Luise Woelflein

sure what happened in the Hawaiian Islands, since no scientists were studying the islands as the new species were introduced. But judging from what is still happening on the islands of Hawaii today, scientists believe that these introduced species contributed to the extinction of much of the native wildlife.

Also point out that the Polynesians and Europeans caused other problems for the native Hawaiian wildlife: They burned and cut down most of the forests to clear the land for farming. And they hunted many of the birds for their meat and feathers.

Explain that plants and animals usually don't cause many problems in the countries they come from. But when they are introduced into areas such as Hawaii, where there are no natural enemies or other ways to control their populations, the introduced species can cause many problems.

Examples of Introduced Species in North America:

water hyacinth
hydrilla
Japanese honeysuckle
kudzu
German cockroach
fire ant
gypsy moth
Japanese beetle
European elm bark
    beetle (carrier of
    Dutch elm disease)
walking catfish
starling
rock dove (pigeon)
English sparrow
house mouse
Norway rat

BRANCHING OUT: INTRODUCED SPECIES WALK

No matter where you live, there are probably a few non-native species right outside your door. You can take your kids on a walk to find these introduced species and talk about how they might be affecting the native species.

Before you go on the walk, call a local authority who can tell you which introduced species are in your area and how they've affected the native species. Nature centers, university departments of

starling

Leonard Lee Rue III

biology, botany, and entomology, and museums of natural history are good places to start looking. (We've also included a short list [in the margin] of introduced species.) You may want to check with a park naturalist to see if he or she would be willing to lead an "introduced species hike" for your group.

Even if you don't see many non-native species on your walk, you can discuss how these species might be affecting the native plants and animals in your area. Here are some points you might want to discuss:

- introduced animals compete with native animals for food and nesting spots
- introduced animals may become pests because they have no natural enemies to control their numbers
- introduced plants compete with native plants for nutrients, sunlight, and other resources
- introduced animals and plants can transmit exotic diseases

41

Short Takes

Read six short articles to learn about some of the reasons that species become endangered.

Objectives:
Name several endangered species. Describe some of the reasons animals and plants become endangered.

Ages:
Intermediate and Advanced

Materials:
- *copies of pages 46 and 47*
- *copies of the questions below*
- *chalkboard or easel paper*

Subjects:
Science and Reading

 here's rarely just one problem that causes an animal or plant to become endangered. Instead, a combination of factors, such as habitat loss, pollution, and so on, usually comes into play. By reading six endangered species "case histories," your kids can learn more about the variety of problems that are causing plants and animals to become endangered.

Before starting the activity, copy the "Case History Questions" we've provided below. (Don't include the answers.) Make enough copies of the questions for the group, then begin the activity by talking about what an endangered species is (see the background information on page 3). Ask the kids if they can think of some of the reasons plants and animals become endangered, and list their answers on a chalkboard or piece of easel paper.

Next pass out copies of pages 46 and 47 to each child. Explain to the kids that as they read the articles, they should take notes about the problems each species is facing. They'll be using these notes later to answer questions about the articles.

Once the kids have finished reading and taking notes, pass out copies of the questions you copied earlier. Tell the kids to put their Copycat Pages away, then have them use their notes to answer the questions. Go over the answers when everyone's finished.

Now ask the kids to again name some of the reasons that species become endangered. Write their reasons down on a chalkboard or piece of easel paper and have the kids compare this second list with the one they made earlier. Then wrap up your discussion by asking the kids if they can name the number one problem that's causing so many species to become endangered. (Habitat destruction is by far the most serious problem animals and plants face today.)

CASE HISTORY QUESTIONS

- **Name some species that are endangered because people like to collect them.** (birdwing butterflies, little agate snails, orchids, Indian pythons)
- **Why do some people in Malaysia think flying foxes are pests? Using the information from the article, explain why you think they're right or wrong.** (Some people think flying foxes eat too much of the fruit people harvest to sell. But studies have shown that flying foxes don't do very much damage after all. And most of the fruit the bats do eat is rotten anyway. Also, flying foxes are important pollinators of fruit trees.)

- **Which of the species in the articles are endangered because of habitat destruction?** (All of them. Most endangered species are affected by habitat destruction in some form. Sometimes the destruction occurs directly, such as when people clear forests to make room for development. [e.g., birdwing butterflies, flying foxes, bald eagles, orchids, and Indian pythons] Other times it's more indirect, such as when introduced plants "take over" a habitat, making it unfit for certain native plants or animals to live there. [e.g., little agate snails])

- **What are some of the problems that caused bald eagles to become endangered?** (pollution from pesticides, lead, and other sources; habitat loss; shot as a "pest")
- **What are the two main reasons that little agate snails are in trouble?** (Non-native species were introduced into their habitat, and people have collected too many of their shells.)
- **From what you've read in these articles, do you think most species are endangered because of only one reason, or because of more than one reason?** (Most species are endangered because of a number of reasons.)

Wildlife for Sale

Make a flip-up page to show that some plants and animals are illegally bought and sold.

Objectives:
Name several plants and animals that are in trouble because of excessive and illegal wildlife trading. Describe some ways people can help stop harmful wildlife trade.

Ages:
Intermediate and Advanced

Materials:
* *copies of pages 48 and 49*
* *crayons or markers*
* *scissors*
* *stapler*
* *sharpened pencils*
* *reference books (optional)*
* *¼ × ¾" (.6 × 1.9-cm) strips of paper (optional)*
* *tape (optional)*

Subject:
Science

 n this activity your kids can make a flip-up page to learn how illegal and excessive wildlife trade can endanger many species. And by learning what *not* to buy, they can help prevent this serious problem.

Begin by passing out copies of pages 48 and 49 to each person. Have them put page 49 aside for now. Then explain that the plants and animals shown on page 48 are endangered or threatened for a number of reasons, but that wildlife trade is one of the main reasons that these species are in trouble. Use the background information under "Tricks of the Trade" on page 34 to explain what wildlife trade is all about. Then have the kids make a flip-up page to reinforce what you discuss. Pass out markers or crayons, pencils, and scissors and have the kids follow the directions below.

1. Color the plant and animal illustrations on page 48. (You can bring out reference books so they can find pictures of the plants and animals. For reference book suggestions, see the bibliography on page 63.)
2. Cut along the dotted lines to make the flaps. (To make cutting easier, have them use sharpened pencils to poke holes through the lines and start cutting from these holes.)
3. Color page 49.
4. Lay the first page (with the flaps) on top of this page and staple the pages together.

Note: You may want to have the kids make tabs for the flaps by taping ¼ × ¾-in (.6 × 1.9-cm) pieces of paper on the bottom edges of the flaps (see diagram in the lower left-hand margin). They can tuck the tabs under to keep the flaps closed.

Now have the kids lift up each flap as you use the information under "Plants and Animals for Sale" to talk about each species and explain what products are made from each animal or plant. To follow up the activity, read the kids a story about parrots in the pet trade. See "A Squawker of My Own" by Claire Miller (*Ranger Rick,* September 1985, pp 8-11).

You can also use the information under "Wildlife Laws and What They Mean" on page 65 to briefly explain to the kids what's been done to help protect these species. Also go over the tips under "What You Can Do" to help kids avoid contributing to the wildlife trade problem.

WHAT YOU CAN DO

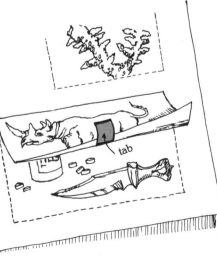

Here are some tips to help you avoid supporting the harmful trade of plants and animals:

* Buy only traditional pets such as dogs, cats, and rabbits. Most wild animals have a difficult time adjusting to life in captivity. (For example, most reptiles and tropical fish soon die in captivity.) Wild animals can also transmit diseases to people and other animals.
* If you do buy a pet bird, stick to captive-bred species such as budgerigars (parakeets), canaries, or cockatiels.
* On trips to other countries, don't buy souvenirs made from sea turtles, spotted cats, or marine mammals. If these products are brought back into the United States, the items will be confiscated and you may be fined.
* Look for cactuses and other plants that appear "perfect"—it's likely that they were not taken from the wild. Wild plants usually have scars and insect damage.
* Be leery of any reptile skin products. It's difficult to tell if the skins were harvested legally.
* Avoid buying coral and ivory jewelry. It's impossible to tell if the materials were collected legally.

For a brochure that explains in more detail what's OK to buy and what's not, write to TRAFFIC(U.S.A.), World Wildlife Fund, 1250 24th St., NW, Washington, DC 20037, and ask for their free "Buyer Beware" booklet. Also ask about their Wildlife Trade Education Kit.

(continued next page)

PLANTS AND ANIMALS FOR SALE

SCARLET MACAW—a type of parrot that lives in tropical forests from Mexico to Brazil; eats fruits, seeds, nuts; endangered because of habitat loss and illegal trade; sold as a pet—each bird sells for about $1500; many of the macaws die during capture and transport; like most other birds that are caught in the wild, usually doesn't make a great pet—bites, sometimes uses its strong beak to destroy wooden perches, and can be extremely noisy; protected—Appendix I, CITES (see page 65 for more about CITES)

GREEN SEA TURTLE—lives in warm oceans all over the world; eats plants and jellyfish; endangered for several reasons (see page 38); meat used for steaks, cartilage for soup, shell for jewelry, eggs for food, oil for cosmetics, skin for leather; endangered

AFRICAN ELEPHANT—lives in African grasslands and forests; eats grasses, leaves, branches, bark, and fruits; estimated 610,000 left in Africa, but populations are decreasing; poaching major reason elephant populations are in trouble, but loss of habitat puts extra pressure on the species; ivory from tusks carved into jewelry or ornaments; elephants must be killed to collect ivory; in October, 1989, CITES nations agreed to ban legal trade in ivory (see page 65 for more about CITES); threatened, but status may soon change to endangered

BLACK CAIMAN—lives in slow-moving rivers in central South America; relative of the American alligator; ambushes animals that come to drink from river; harvested for skin—usually only soft underbelly skin is used; also shot by people who consider it a threat to livestock; endangered

SNOW LEOPARD—lives in remote mountainous areas in central Asia; eats mountain goats, deer, sheep, marmots, and other animals; spotted coat in demand for fur coats; also killed by trophy hunters and by people who consider it a threat to livestock; most fur coats marketed in Japan and West Germany; endangered

LIVING ROCK CACTUS—grows in single desert valley in Mexico; grows to a height of only 2 inches (5 cm); its name comes from its close resemblance to rocks; dug up by private collectors and by commercial dealers; bought by collectors of rare and unusual plants; can be grown commercially, but much easier and less costly for dealers to take from wild; protected—Appendix I, CITES

CORALS—small animals that live in colonies in shallow, tropical waters; eat tiny sea plants and animals; limestone skeletons of dead corals form reefs; living corals give reefs their brilliant colors; reefs support great variety of life, also reduce erosion of beaches; some coral collected for jewelry and souvenir trade; used in building and to make lime for fertilizer; dynamite sometimes used to blast apart huge chunks of reef; coral in some areas can be collected legally, but once imported into the United States, can't be distinguished from illegal coral; protected—Appendix II, CITES

BLACK RHINOCEROS—lives in central and southern Africa; browses on branches and twigs; threatened by habitat destruction as more land is cleared for farms; killed for its horn which can sell for thousands of dollars a pound (horn from Asian species even more expensive); horns are in great demand in North Yemen, where they're carved into handles for traditional daggers; horns also ground into powder and added to Asian medicines; endangered

SPERM WHALE—found in oceans all around the world (except for northernmost polar seas); males can grow up to 60 feet (18 m) long (about the length of 2 school buses) and weigh 70 tons (63 t); eats mostly squid, also octopus, fish, shrimp; harvested for a waxy material that is used to lubricate machinery and to make cosmetics, skin cream, and perfume; teeth used for scrimshaw carvings; although most harvesting has stopped, population is still low; endangered

Leonard Lee Rue III

African bull elephant

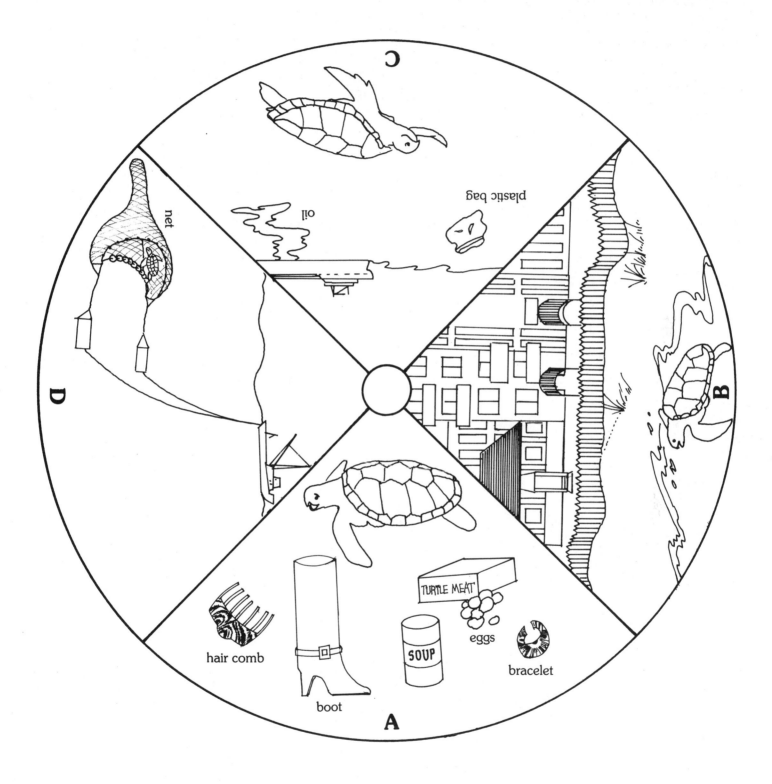

A

hair comb

boot

TURTLE MEAT

SOUP

eggs

bracelet

B

C

plastic bag

oil

net

D

BIRDWING BUTTERFLIES

Picture a shimmering, yellow-and-black butterfly the size of a robin. That's what one of the birdwing butterflies looks like. Birdwings are some of the biggest and brightest butterflies in the world. Most of them live in warm parts of the world such as Papua New Guinea, Malaysia, and Australia.

Many people like to collect birdwings because of their size and beauty. Sometimes people preserve the entire butterfly, but others use just the wings as decorations. (Collecting doesn't cause most species of butterflies to become endangered. But it is a problem for birdwings because they are naturally rare and they reproduce slowly.)

But the biggest problem birdwings face is the loss of the forests where they live. These forests are being destroyed to make room for farms, houses, or other development.

LITTLE AGATE SNAILS

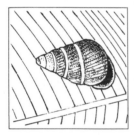

Little agate snails are among the most colorful creatures in all of Hawaii. They're also among the rarest.

Problems started for these tiny snails when animals such as other kinds of snails and rats were brought to Hawaii. These new predators ate many of the little agate snails.

Certain plants that people brought to Hawaii also caused problems. The plants spread and replaced many of the native shrubs and trees little agate snails needed for food.

Another problem little agate snails have faced is overcollecting. People have collected hundreds of thousands of their beautiful shells. Today there are very few of the little agate snails left in Hawaii.

FLYING FOXES

Most foxes keep their feet on the ground—but some "foxes" actually fly! These flying "foxes" aren't really foxes, though. They're certain species of bats that live in Africa and Southeast Asia and on islands in the Indian and Pacific Oceans. They're named for their foxlike faces.

Flying foxes eat fruit, as well as nectar and pollen. In some places people kill the bats because they think the animals eat too much fruit. (Many people in these areas harvest fruit for a living.) But scientists have discovered that the bats really don't eat very much of the fruit that people harvest. And any fruit they do eat is usually rotten. Scientists have also discovered that many of these bats help pollinate the fruit trees as they feed.

Besides being shot because they eat fruit, many species of flying foxes are also hunted for their tasty meat. And many are losing their homes because people are chopping down forests for firewood or to clear land for farms.

(See Short Takes—p 42)

BALD EAGLE

Most Americans recognize the bald eagle as the symbol of our country. But many don't know that bald eagles were once thought of as pests that killed chickens and other livestock. Because of this belief, people shot thousands of eagles.

Today it's illegal to shoot eagles. But the birds are facing many other problems. For example, they've lost much of their habitat to roads, housing projects, and other development.

Pollution has also hurt eagles. Lead, pesticides, and other pollutants build up in the tissues of the animals that the eagles eat. And when the eagles eat these poisoned animals, they often become poisoned too.

ORCHIDS

Orchids are among the most beautiful flowers in the world. There are many different kinds of orchids, and a lot of them are in trouble. One reason is that many of the forests and other areas where these plants grow are being cleared for farms, houses, and other development.

Another problem is overcollecting. Some people gather orchids for their private collections. Others dig up the plants and sell them. (Most orchids are hard to grow indoors, so it's easier for people to take them from the wild.)

Even orchids that grow on the branches of tropical trees, high up in the forest, aren't safe. That's because some collectors cut down the trees these orchids live on to collect the rare flowers.

INDIAN PYTHON

Imagine a snake that's 20 feet (6 m) long and weighs 200 pounds (90 kg)! That's the size of a large Indian python. This snake lives in India and Sri Lanka.

During the last 10 years or so, there has been a big push to collect unusual animals and sell them as pets. And Indian pythons have been one of the "hottest" items. People have collected so many of these snakes that very few are left in the wild. And the pythons that *are* left are having a hard time surviving. That's because people are bringing more and more cattle into the pythons' habitat. The cattle are overgrazing the areas where pythons live.

Many pythons are also caught and skinned to make shoes, boots, and belts, despite the fact that it's illegal to kill these snakes.

(See Short Takes—p 42)

WILDLIFE FOR SALE—SHEET 1

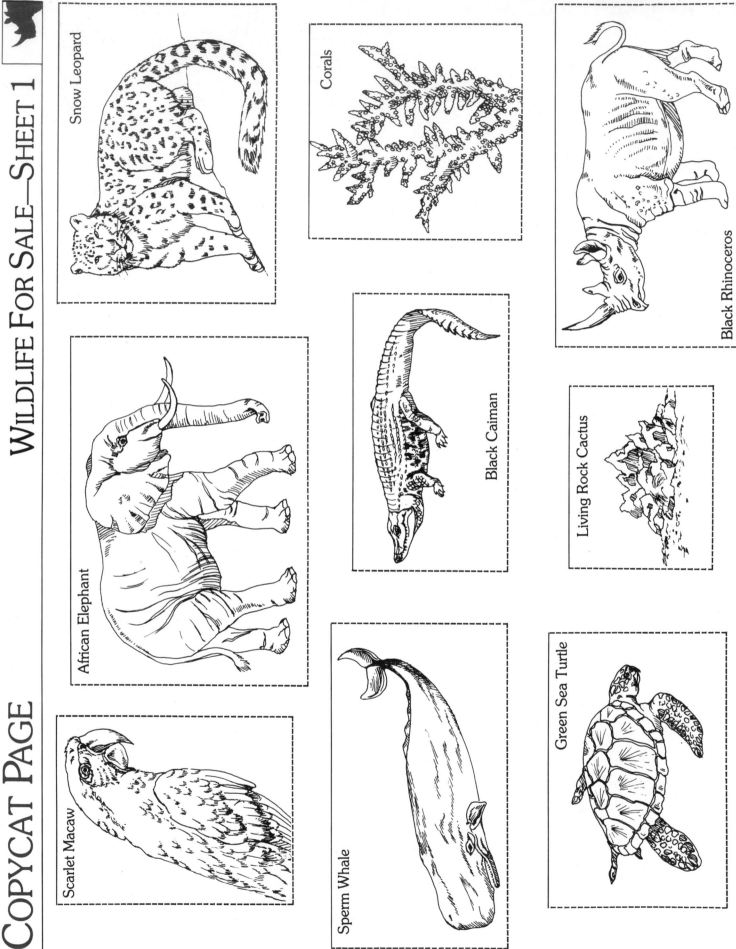

Snow Leopard

Corals

Black Rhinoceros

African Elephant

Black Caiman

Living Rock Cactus

Scarlet Macaw

Sperm Whale

Green Sea Turtle

RANGER RICK'S NATURESCOPE: ENDANGERED SPECIES—WILD AND RARE
(See *Wildlife for Sale*—p 43)

COPYCAT PAGE

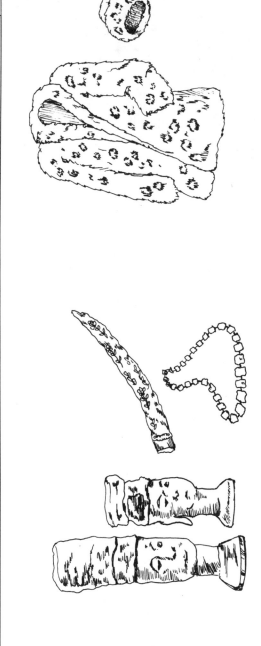

LIME

PILLS

MACHINE OIL

COLD CREAM

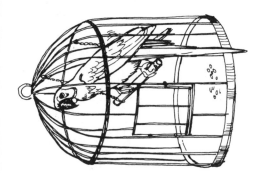

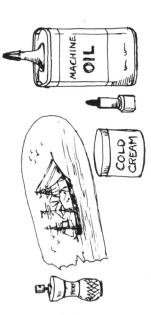

SOUP CREAM OF TURTLE

TURTLE MEAT

RANGER RICK'S NATURESCOPE: ENDANGERED SPECIES—WILD AND RARE
(See *Wildlife for Sale*—p 43)

BOUNCING BACK

L ate in 1983 scientists tried an experiment. They flew a group of golden lion tamarins—one of the most endangered mammals in the world—to Brazil to see if they could successfully release them into their native habitat. The scientists knew that these little lion monkeys, born and raised in a zoo far from their wild home, had a lot to learn before they could be set free in the forest. So for a while the fiery-colored, squirrel-sized primates lived in outdoor cages and learned about their new home.

Finally, the tamarins were released. And since their release, some of the survivors have raised families in the wild. Although golden lion tamarins are still seriously endangered, the success scientists have had with them means there's hope for their survival. The tamarin project, and many others that are in progress, demonstrate some of the ways people can help animals and plants survive in a world where human-caused extinctions are on the rise.

A HELPING HAND

Some endangered species don't need much direct help from people. If the problem threatening them with extinction is removed and they're left alone in the wild, they can often take care of themselves. But a "let-them-alone" policy isn't effective enough to save some animals and plants. The particular problems affecting a species, combined with things like the species' breeding cycle, how much room it needs to live, and what kind of food it eats, sometimes make survival impossible without intensive efforts by people.

Survival Centers: In the last 20 years or so, the "art" of breeding animals and propagating plants in captivity has emerged as one way of helping endangered species survive. Ultimately, the goal of most captive reproduction programs for endangered species is to build up the species' numbers.

Sometimes special centers are set up to increase the numbers of one or more endangered species. But zoos and botanical gardens are the most important sites for breeding animals and propagating plants. And as more and more species become endangered, the role of zoos and botanical gardens in trying to prevent extinctions will become much more visible. The efforts of these institutions, however, will never be able to compensate for the large numbers of species that are becoming endangered or extinct because of habitat loss.

Some Are Flexible, Others Are "Finicky": With some species, such as certain types of deer and other grazers, captive reproduction is usually a simple enough procedure. Scientists don't have to do much more than make sure males and females are both in the same area at the same time. Other species, though, aren't so "accommodating." These species usually have very specialized needs: a strict diet during the breeding season, a particular type of weather, a certain amount of daylight in relation to darkness, and so on.

Building Up the Numbers: Getting species to reproduce on their own in captivity (or in the wild, for that matter) isn't always the most efficient way to increase their numbers—especially since some species breed very infrequently and/or have only one or two young at one time. And since some species can't afford to "dawdle" (their numbers are just too low), scientists have developed ways to help them along. By using artificial insemination, for example, scientists can often produce young of certain animals several times in a single year. (Left to their own devices,

golden lion tamarin

these species would produce far fewer offspring in the same period of time.) Scientists are also trying many other techniques, such as using closely related species as surrogate mothers and freezing sperm and embryos for later use.

NUMBER ONE PRIORITIES

Of course, any efforts to boost a species' numbers won't mean much in the future if the habitat of an animal or plant doesn't exist or if the area is too degraded to support the species. As we pointed out in "All Around the World" on page 25, habitat protection is ultimately the key to saving endangered species.

This fact becomes especially clear when you consider just how limited zoos and other breeding facilities are: The combined efforts of all such facilities around the world—even if they put into action the latest in captive reproduction "technology"—could help only a tiny fraction of the thousands of species that are in trouble now. And as habitats shrink, more and more species will be needing all the help they can get.

Steps in the Right Direction: Fortunately, some habitat has been set aside in the form of parks, wildlife refuges, and other reserves. Around the world, more than 3500 protected areas exist, covering a total of about two million square miles (5 million km^2).

Still, that's only three percent of the world's total land area. And many existing reserves are proving too small to support healthy populations of some of the animals that live there. But researchers are starting to learn more about the specific habitat requirements of different species, including the amount of space different species need. Once they determine the requirements of species that are endangered or threatened, they can make recommendations on how large the reserves containing these species should be.

Undoing the Damage: Protecting species through habitat preservation is difficult when original habitats have been severely altered. But a new approach—habitat restoration—may help to reverse at least a little of the damage that has been done.

At this point, habitat restoration projects are rare. Putting an area back into its original form can be difficult and expensive. And the expertise and technology needed to "fix" certain habitat types are sometimes limited or nonexistent. But some of the projects now being conducted look pretty encouraging. For example, ecologists in Costa Rica are training local people to plant and manage a tropical forest that had been degraded by cattle ranching. If this works, it could mean that thousands of acres of overgrazed tropical lands in Central and South America could be restored.

The Push to Protect: For a lot of reasons—political, economic, and ecological, to name a few—efforts to save species and their habitats have almost always been struggles against tough odds. But ingenuity and commitment, along with a little luck, have given us some encouraging results. Golden lion tamarins, bald eagles, and others are doing better now than they were just a few years ago.

These successes are the result of a growing trend: an increasing desire—and need—to protect what we have. Out of this "push to protect" has come an increasing number of important laws and regulations, from the creation of new parks, refuges, and other reserves to the crackdown on wildlife trafficking. (For more about laws protecting endangered species, see page 65.)

They're Bouncing Back!

Learn about some endangered species' success stories by "performing" a chant with motions.

Objectives:
Name several species that are doing better now than they once were. Discuss some of the problems these species have faced and the ways people have helped them.

Ages:
Primary

Materials:
- *pictures of whooping cranes, alligators, bald eagles, and polar bears*

Subject:
Science

There's so much bad news associated with endangered species and the increasing rate of extinction that it's easy to overlook the positive things that have happened. Many people don't realize, for example, that bald eagles are doing much better now than they were just a few years ago. So are whooping cranes and alligators. Pronghorn antelope, American bison, trumpeter swans, and many other species are also better off now than they once were.

Here's an active way for young kids to learn about some of these endangered species' success stories. First discuss each of the four species listed under "Success Stories" (at the end of the activity). Use the information we've provided to briefly go over the problems each species has faced and how the animal has been helped. Also show the kids pictures of the animals during your discussion.

Afterward, get the kids up on their feet and have them form a circle. Go over the motions and words of the following chant, then have the kids "perform" the chant a couple of times as they march around the circle. You might want to add a few verses of your own too—see the list on page 55 for some other examples of species that are doing better than they once were.

Ellen Lambeth

THEY'RE BOUNCING BACK!

Words:	**Motions:**
They're bouncing back, They're bouncing back, The whooping cranes are bouncing back! Tall and graceful birds that dance, Now they have another chance.	Slowly flap arms up and down and lift legs high with each step.
They're bouncing back, etc. The gators now are bouncing back! Sharp-toothed beasts with scaly skin, They're swimming in the swamps again.	Stretch arms out in front and move them apart and together to imitate jaws opening and closing.
They're bouncing back, etc. Bald eagles now are bouncing back! Soaring over lake and bay, Doing better every day.	Hold arms straight out to side and lean this way and that as though soaring.
They're bouncing back, etc. The polar bears are bouncing back! Snowy white with coal-black eyes, Their numbers now are on the rise.	Hold arms up in front of you with fingers curled, and move forearms up and down.

Whooping crane—In 1945, there were only 19 whooping cranes left in the world. Their numbers had dwindled to this point for a couple of reasons. One was that the big white birds made easy targets, causing many cranes to be shot. Another problem the cranes faced was the depletion of their habitat: Many of the marshy areas they lived in were drained and filled to create farms and housing developments.

Finally, though, habitat was set aside for whooping cranes and captive breeding efforts got underway. Now there are about 200 birds. Whoopers are still endangered, but people's efforts have made their future look much brighter than it once did. (For more information about cranes, see page 59.)

Alligator—These wetland reptiles weren't doing too well back in the 1960s, when there was a high demand for alligator shoes, belts, purses, and other products made from alligator leather. But the Endangered Species Act of 1973 made it illegal to sell alligator skins, and the animals recovered quickly. Now, throughout much of their range, alligators are no longer considered endangered.

Bald eagle—Many populations of these birds have been increasing steadily since the mid-1970s. Before that time, eagles were in trouble mainly because of DDT. This pesticide accumulated in the birds' bodies, poisoning some outright and causing many eagles to lay eggs with very thin shells. Most of these thin-shelled eggs broke under the weight of the incubating parent birds.

DDT was banned from most uses in the United States in 1972. Since then, there have been intensive efforts to protect eagle habitat and breed the birds in captivity. By all indications, bald eagles are now making a comeback.

Polar bear—In the mid-1960s, a research team made up of scientists from several nations concluded that too many polar bears were being killed for their meat, their fur, and/or sport. Some feared that if the polar bear harvest wasn't controlled, the animals would be extinct within a decade. The scientists came up with suggestions for saving the bear, recommending that the harvest be limited to bears taken by native peoples using traditional weapons and hunting techniques. Since this policy went into effect, the bears have been doing better in many areas.

People Power

Become involved in a project to help endangered species.

Objective:
Name some of the ways individuals and groups can help endangered species.

Ages:
All

Subjects:
Science and Social Studies

People often feel there's not much they can do to help endangered species. The problems these species face, after all, are sometimes very complicated, involving not only the animal or plant itself but also factors such as politics, cultural tradition, and economics. But many individuals and citizens' groups have done a lot to help endangered species.

The King Oak Nature Club of Oak Creek Elementary School in Houston, Texas, is a great example of what kids can do for endangered species. For several years, this club has worked hard to help the endangered Kemp's ridley sea turtle. Their project is called HEART (Help Endangered Animals—Ridley Turtles). Among other things, HEART raises money to buy food for young Kemp's ridleys that are being raised in captivity for later release. It raises enough money, in fact, to help scientists hatch and raise nearly 2000 Kemp's ridleys each year!

There are several ways you and your kids can help HEART do its work. For one thing, you can make a contribution of $4.00—the amount required to feed a hatchling turtle for one year. Or you can form a HEART Council by contributing $20.00 or more, writing to federal legislators, and viewing a special video about the Kemp's ridley.

There are many other projects and organizations your kids can contribute to, as well. (See the list on the next page.) Some of these projects and organizations allow you to "adopt" an endangered animal for a certain fee. "Adoptive parents" usually receive photos, progress reports, and other information about their animals.) But you might prefer to do what the HEART kids did and start your own project. One of the best ways to do this is to find out about species needing help in your area.

Local nature centers and conservation groups may be able to give you some information about endangered species in your community or state. They might also be able to let you know about endangered species research projects and other efforts your group could raise money for. Your kids might even be able to do some volunteer work for a local endangered species effort. But whatever way you choose to get involved, you and your group *can* make a difference!

Recovery!

Read a comic strip about ospreys, create a comic strip about whooping cranes, and draw a picture of an animal that has "bounced back" from the edge of extinction.

Objectives:
Describe some of the ways people help endangered species. Name some plants and animals that were once nearly extinct, but are now doing better.

Ages:
Intermediate and Advanced

Materials:
- *copies of pages 58 and 59*
- *chalkboard or easel paper*
- *crayons or markers*
- *index cards*
- *construction paper*
- *drawing paper*

 he whooping crane, red wolf, Kemp's ridley sea turtle, and hundreds of other species in the United States are listed as endangered or threatened. The goal of the U.S. Fish and Wildlife Service, which oversees the U.S. endangered species list and the nation's endangered species program, is to restore these "listed" plants and animals to the point where their populations are self-sustaining and the species are no longer in danger of becoming extinct. To do that, the Fish and Wildlife Service develops a specific recovery plan for each species. The recovery plan identifies what needs to be done to help the species, how it will be done, and when it will be done.

In the first part of this two-part activity, your group will find out about some of the ways people help species that are in trouble. In the second part, they'll learn about several species that are doing better now than they once were.

PART 1: ON THE COMEBACK TRAIL

Start this part of the activity by discussing how people go about helping a species that's in trouble. Explain that once an animal or plant is listed as endangered or threatened, scientists work together to come up with a recovery plan. To carry out such a plan, scientists must first do research to find out why the species is in trouble and what it needs in order to avoid extinction.

Stress that because different types of plants and animals have different prob-lems, each species has a unique recovery plan. But many of the general components of a recovery plan are similar for different species. For example, most recovery plans stress the importance of habitat protection, public education, and strict enforcement of laws.

After your discussion, show the kids pictures of ospreys and pass out a copy of page 58 to each person. Have the kids read the comic strip to find out why the osprey was in trouble and what scientists did to help it recover. (You might want to explain what DDT is and discuss the fact that it can get into animals' tissues. Explain that this pesticide was sprayed on crops, gardens, and wetlands to kill insects, and it caused many problems for certain fish, birds, and other animals.) When the kids have finished reading, ask them to name what some of the osprey's problems were and list their answers on a chalkboard or sheet of easel paper. Also list some of the ways scientists and others have helped ospreys make a comeback.

Next show the kids pictures of whooping cranes and pass out copies of page 59. Explain that the article on the page is about the whooping crane, an endangered bird that lives in North America. Have the kids read the page and then use the information in the article to create their own whooping crane comic strips. Afterward, talk about the problems whooping cranes have faced and the ways scientists are helping them recover.

PART 2: THE SUCCESS HALL OF FAME

CANDIDATES FOR THE SUCCESS HALL OF FAME

alligator
American bison
Arabian oryx
bald eagle
brown pelican
cougar
eastern bluebird
elephant seal
elk
European bison (wisent)
golden lion tamarin
gray whale
Hawaiian goose
Hawaiian monk seal
koala
masked bobwhite
musk ox
northern sea otter
osprey
Père David's deer
peregrine falcon
polar bear
pronghorn antelope
saguaro cactus
snowy egret
teosinte
trumpeter swan
vicuña
whimbrel
whooping crane
wild turkey
wood duck

Before starting this part of the activity, copy each animal or plant name in the margin onto a separate slip of paper and put the slips in a sack. Then have each child draw one slip from the sack.

Explain that the animals they've picked are examples of species that are doing better now than they once were. (Some are doing better than others, though many are still listed as endangered. But all are facing a brighter future than they were before.) Explain that each person must try to find out why his or her plant or animal was in trouble and how people have helped it recover. (Tell them to take notes on the information they find.)

After the kids finish researching, have them draw a picture of their species on a piece of paper and frame the picture with a piece of colored construction paper. They could also make paper-mache models of the animals or plants or use paint, chalk, or some other medium to make the portraits. Have them write the names of their animals or plants in big, bold letters on index cards.

When everyone is finished, hang the portraits on a wall, with the name of each species underneath the portrait. Title the display "THE SUCCESS HALL OF FAME." Then have each person give a short speech to the rest of the group explaining why his or her species deserves to be in the Success Hall of Fame.

Harry Engels

trumpeter swan

Meet the Press

Hold a "press conference" about people who have helped endangered species, then write news articles.

Objectives:
Name several species whose populations have increased because of help from people. Describe some of the ways people have helped these species.

Ages:
Advanced

Materials:
- *writing paper*
- *pens or pencils*
- *copy of "People Who Made a Difference" on page 57*
- *chalkboard or easel paper*
- *cardboard or heavy paper*
- *table*
- *reference books (optional)*
- *pictures of cranes, key deer, and trumpeter swans (optional)*
- *microphone (optional)*
- *crayons or markers (optional)*
- *drawing paper (optional)*

Subjects:
Science and Language Arts

 ry this activity to give your kids a chance to "meet" some of the special people who've given certain endangered species a helping hand. First copy the information under "People Who Made a Difference" (next page) and cut the three articles apart. Then introduce the activity by telling the kids that they'll be taking part in a "press conference" that will focus on a few of the many people who have worked hard to save animals in trouble.

Next choose three kids (or let the kids volunteer) to play the parts of Glenn Allen, Trudy Edwards, and George Archibald. Pass out to the appropriate people the articles you copied earlier. The rest of the kids will make up the "press corps." Their job during the conference will be to ask the endangered species' "helpers" questions about the species they've worked with and how they helped the animals survive.

Now give the kids time to prepare for the conference. Tell the role players to carefully go over the information you gave them, and encourage them to do a little extra research on their own. (See the end of the activity for a list of *Ranger Rick* articles that might be helpful.) You might want to suggest that the role players jot down notes for use during the conference, and you could also have them draw or find pictures of their animals.

To get ready for their part in the conference, the press corps kids should try to come up with the questions they'll be asking the three role players at the press conference. Explain that they'll be taking notes based on these questions during the conference, and they'll use these notes later to write news articles. To help the kids along, ask them what kinds of questions they think they should ask. (Tell them to keep in mind that the articles they'll be writing should answer some of the basic questions readers might have about the people and endangered species involved.) List the kids' suggestions on a chalkboard or sheet of easel paper, and add any others you feel are important.

Here are a few sample questions you might want to have the kids include:
- Which endangered species have you worked with?
- Why did the animal become endangered?
- Where did you do your work?
- How did you get started?
- What did you do to help?

Make sure the kids' questions are in a place where everyone can see them, and encourage the role players to look them over so they'll know what to expect at the press conference.

When you're ready to hold the conference, have the role players sit at a table facing the rest of the group. (You might want to use a microphone as a prop.) Write the name of the person each role player represents, along with the species he or she has helped, on a piece of cardboard or heavy paper and prop it up in front of the role player. Then get the conference started by having the three role players tell a little about themselves. For example, the person playing Trudy Edwards could mention that she first started helping the swans when she was 12 and that she now has a daughter helping her. If the role players have pictures of their animals, you could have them hold the pictures up as they introduce themselves.

Now have the kids take turns asking one question at a time. You might want to act as "press secretary" so you can moderate the questioning and see that everyone gets a chance to participate. At the end of the conference, assign each of the press corps kids one of the three endangered species' helpers to write about. (Remind them that their articles should include answers to the questions they asked during the conference.) The role players themselves should write "autobiographical sketches" that include information about how they've helped endangered species.

Ranger Rick Articles:
- "Swans" and "Toy Deer Bounce Back" (June 1984)
- "Crazy About Cranes" and "Crane Crazy Kids" (April 1983)

Glenn Allen worked long and hard to help save Florida's *key deer*. These tiny deer live only on the islands off the tip of Florida called the Keys.

When Glenn started his project to help key deer in 1949, he was 11 years old. At that time, only a few dozen of the animals were left. The deer were in trouble because so many people had moved into the Keys. Much of the deer's habitat had been cleared to make room for homes and canals. And many of the deer had been killed for their meat.

The first thing Glenn did to help the deer was to learn all he could about them. Then for the next eight years he wrote letters and talked to people about the deer's problems. He wrote to Presidents Truman and Eisenhower to ask that land be set aside for the deer. He also wrote to other officials and to newspapers. Florida's government did pass a law to stop people from killing the deer, but Glenn knew this wasn't enough. He knew the animals needed a protected area of land—a refuge—that people wouldn't be allowed to disturb. But at that time no refuge was set up.

By the time Glenn was 19, many people had learned about the key deer problem and wanted to help. Congress thought about the refuge Glenn had asked for. This time *lots* of kids and adults all across the country wrote letters saying they wanted the refuge. Congress voted "yes" and established the National Key Deer Refuge. Today the tiny deer are doing much better than they once were, but they still need people's help to survive.

Trudy Edwards was only 12 years old when she began taking care of a small flock of *trumpeter swans*. In the 1800s the huge swans had been killed in great numbers for their feathers and skins. By the 1920s, when Trudy's father discovered a small group at Lonesome Lake in Canada, many people felt the trumpeters were in danger of becoming extinct. The Canadian government supplied Trudy's family with grain to feed the rare birds on Lonesome Lake. It became Trudy's job to take food down to the lake each day during the winter. If the swans hadn't been fed, many of them might have starved.

Now Trudy is grown up and has a daughter of her own. But she still feeds trumpeter swans on Lonesome Lake. They know her and wait for her every day. The Lonesome Lake flock has grown from about 35 birds to more than 400. And programs in other parts of Canada and the U.S. have helped raise the total number of these swans to more than 12,000. Now trumpeters—the largest swans in the world—are no longer endangered.

George Archibald, a scientist who studies birds, has done a lot to help *whooping cranes* and other endangered cranes. One reason some cranes are in trouble is that so much of their wetland habitat has been drained and filled in to make way for farms, houses, and other types of development.

George helped to set up the International Crane Foundation, an organization that is working hard to save the world's 15 crane species. One thing the Foundation has done is to breed cranes in captivity and release the young birds into the wild. George has helped develop ways to get the captive cranes to breed. Sometimes the methods are complicated. But sometimes all it takes is a little trick. For example, if the captive cranes are from a country that has lots of monsoon rains, George sprinkles them with water so they'll feel at home. When the birds feel at home, they're more likely to mate and lay eggs.

One of the most important things George does now is to work with other countries to help them protect their own cranes. One way he does this is by helping scientists in other countries find and preserve important crane habitat. So far he has helped set aside land for cranes in India, Japan, Korea, China, and Vietnam.

The Whooping Cranes' Story

Many birds can sing. But whooping cranes are "talented" in another way: They can dance! To get ready for the nesting season, these graceful white birds dance by bowing, flapping their wings, and jumping into the air.

Once these dancing birds nearly became extinct. But scientists and other people have worked hard to help them survive. And although whooping cranes are still an endangered species, they're doing better now than they once were.

Whooping cranes live in marshy areas. They wade through the water on their long legs, searching for small fish, crabs, and other water animals to eat. And they build their nests among the marsh plants.

The cranes became endangered for a couple of reasons. For one thing, the marshes where whoopers lived were filled in to make room for crops and houses. Also, many cranes were accidentally shot. (In flight, whooping cranes can look like certain kinds of geese and other birds that people hunt.) By the 1940s, there were only about 20 whooping cranes left.

One of the first things people did to help the cranes was to set aside some land for them. This area, the Aransas (uh-RAN-sus) National Wildlife Refuge in Texas, is the cranes' winter home. But scientists hadn't yet discovered where the birds went in spring and summer to breed and raise their young.

While scientists were looking for the cranes' breeding grounds, many people were doing other things to help the cranes. For example, to try to keep people from shooting whooping cranes by mistake, officials helped people learn how to recognize them.

Then in the 1950s, scientists finally found the whooping cranes' breeding grounds. It turns out that the birds fly to a small area in Canada to lay eggs and raise their young. Once scientists knew where the cranes went to breed, they could learn more about the birds and their nesting habits.

In the late 1960s scientists decided to try something new to help the whoopers. They decided to start a project to increase the crane's numbers faster than the birds could do on their own. Whooping cranes usually lay two eggs in the spring. Often both eggs hatch. But most of the time only one of the chicks survives. So for several years starting in 1967, scientists collected one of the two eggs from each whooping crane nest. They sent these eggs to a research center and put them in incubators.

When the whooping crane chicks hatched, people fed and took care of them. Many of these chicks grew up healthy and strong. And many of them mated and laid their own eggs. Before too long there was a healthy population of whooping cranes at the research center.

In 1975, the scientists tried another experiment. First they gathered up some of the eggs laid by the birds at the research center. Then they shipped the eggs to an area in Idaho. Here, a non-endangered whooping crane relative—the sandhill crane—nests. Workers put the whooper eggs into the nests of the sandhills. And just as they had hoped, these cranes raised the whooping crane chicks as their own. In this way the sandhill cranes became foster parents to the young cranes. And when the sandhills flew to their wintering area in New Mexico, the young whoopers flew right along with them. Now there were two flocks of whooping cranes: The "original" flock at Aransas and the "new" one that lived with the sandhills.

Scientists are still raising whooping cranes and using sandhill cranes as foster parents. And their efforts seem to be paying off. Now there are more than 200 whoopers. That's more than eight times as many as there were back in the early 1940s!

CRAFTY CORNER

Panda Pals

*Make a panda mask
and a panda puppet.*

*Ages:
Primary and
Intermediate*

*Materials:
See separate lists un-
der directions for mask
and puppet.*

*Subjects:
Arts and Crafts*

Pandas are irresistible—especially to kids! Here are a couple of panda crafts your group is sure to have fun with.

HOW TO MAKE A PANDA MASK

(You'll need a white paper plate, a quarter, a black marker, black construction paper, scissors, a paper punch, a stapler, and some string.)

1. Turn a paper plate over so that the bottom faces up. Trace around a quarter to make two eye holes. They should be in the center of the plate, about 2 inches (5 cm) apart. Cut out the holes.
2. Draw in the nose and the patches around the panda's eyes. Color them in with a black marker.
3. Cut a snout shape under the nose that tapers up into the sides of the face.
4. Cut out two ears from black construction paper. Staple them onto the top of the mask.
5. Punch a hole on each side of the mask and tie one piece of string to each hole.
6. To wear the mask, have someone tie the two strings together in back of your head. Adjust the knot so that you're able to slip the mask on and off easily.

Note: For younger children, make cardboard ear and snout patterns so they have something to trace around.

cut out eye hole

punch hole and attach string

cut off bottom of plate to make a snout

HOW TO MAKE A PANDA PUPPET

glue head to sock

cut out hole

glue legs to sock

(You'll need a white sock, a piece of thin white cardboard, glue, a black marker, a black glove, and scissors.)

1. Draw a panda's face (about 3½ inches [9 cm] in diameter) on thin white cardboard and cut it out. (Refer to the shape and design of the panda mask when drawing the puppet's face.) Color in the panda's eyes and nose.
2. Cut two ears out of the cardboard, color them black, and glue them onto the panda's head.
3. Draw and cut out two hind legs from the cardboard and color them black. Lay the legs aside for now.
4. Cut a hole on each side of the sock, about 3 inches (8 cm) from the toe. (When you later put the puppet on

your hand, your thumb should be able to fit through one hole and your little finger through the other.)

5. Glue the panda's head to the toe of the sock. Place glue only at the top of the head, allowing the head to move freely.
6. Glue the panda's legs in place about 2 inches (5 cm) below the finger holes.
7. Let the puppet dry.

8. To give your panda a more "realistic" look, you might want to color in or paint on the black band that runs around the panda's chest and back.
9. Put on a black glove, then pull the sock over the glove. Slide your thumb and little finger through the holes in the sock. Now move your fingers and thumb around to make your puppet nod, wave, and gesture.

These Cards Say a Mouthful!

Make pop-up cards of endangered species.

Ages:
Intermediate and Advanced

Materials:
- *8½ × 11" pieces of white paper*
- *scissors*
- *glue*
- *crayons, markers, or colored pencils*
- *pictures of endangered animals*

Subjects:
Arts and Crafts

Your kids can help spread the word about animals in danger by making and sending endangered species pop-up cards. Here's how to make one:
1. Fold an 8½ × 11-inch piece of paper in half lengthwise.
2. About a quarter of the way down on the fold, cut a 1½-inch (4-cm) slit (see diagram 1).
3. Fold the paper back from the slit into small triangles (see diagram 2).
4. Unfold the paper, then fold it in half widthwise so that the slit faces you (see diagram 3).
5. Pull the top and bottom of the slit outward and fold the paper in half again

(see diagram 4). Work with the card to make the top and bottom of the slit open and close like a mouth.
6. Draw and color an animal's face around the "mouth." If you draw an endangered bird, such as the Philippine eagle we've pictured, you might want to glue on a paper beak (see diagram 5). And for wolves, leopards, or other endangered mammal predators, you could add sharp teeth.
7. Write messages in your card. (You can even put a message inside the animal's mouth!)

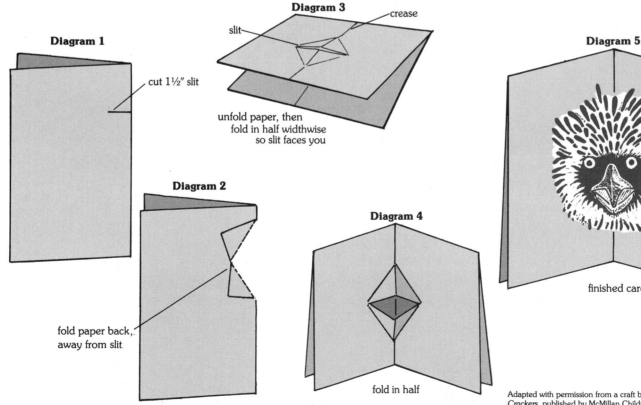

Diagram 1

cut 1½" slit

Diagram 2

fold paper back, away from slit

Diagram 3

crease

slit

unfold paper, then fold in half widthwise so slit faces you

Diagram 4

fold in half

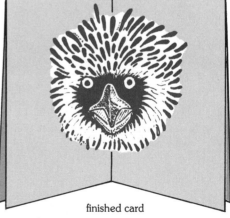

Diagram 5

finished card

Adapted with permission from a craft by Colin Caket in *Christmas Crackers*, published by McMillan Children's Books.

APPENDIX

Glossary

acid rain—a type of pollution that occurs when sulfur and nitrogen compounds in the atmosphere react with water vapor. The rain that forms from this vapor is acidic and can damage forests, aquatic organisms, crops, buildings, and other things.

adaptation—a behavior, physical feature, or other characteristic that helps an animal or plant survive and make the most of its habitat. For example, the saguaro cactus, which lives in the desert, can store water. This adaptation helps it survive through periods of drought.

biological diversity—the diversity of life on Earth, reflected in the number and variety of species and populations, and the communities that they form.

community—a group of interacting plants and animals living in the same area.

endangered species—a species that is in immediate danger of becoming extinct. The black rhinoceros is an endangered species.

extinct—no longer living. The Carolina parakeet is an extinct species.

habitat—the area where an animal or plant lives and finds nutrients, water, shelter, and living space.

introduced species—an animal or plant species that has been brought into areas where the species never lived before. For example, people brought starlings to North America from Europe. Introduced species often compete with and cause problems for native species. (Introduced species are also called *exotic* or *non-native species*.)

market hunting—the hunting or trapping of animals to sell for profit. For example, bison were often hunted for their hides, which were shipped east for sale.

native species—a species that occurs naturally in an area.

population—an interbreeding group of animals or plants of the same species that lives in the same area.

poach—to hunt, kill, or collect a plant or animal illegally.

overgrazing—the process that occurs when cattle, sheep, goats, or other animals graze in too small an area for too long a period. Overgrazing often results in soil erosion, the destruction of vegetation, and other problems.

rare species—a species that has a small number of individuals and/or has a limited distribution. A rare species may or may not be endangered or threatened. The kakapo, a New Zealand parrot, is a rare species. (It is also endangered.)

threatened species—a species whose numbers are low or declining. A threatened species is not in immediate danger of extinction, but it is likely to become endangered if it isn't protected. The African elephant is a threatened species.

Bibliography

(Note: A ✒ at the end of a listing indicates that a book is a good source of endangered species pictures.)

GENERAL REFERENCE BOOKS

The Doomsday Book of Animals by David Day (Viking Press, 1981) ✒
Endangered Species Handbook by Greta Nilsson (Animal Welfare Institute, 1986). One copy is free to educators. Write Animal Welfare Institute, P.O. Box 2650, Washington, DC 20007.
Extinction by Paul and Anne Ehrlich (Random House, 1981)
From the Edge of Extinction by Darryl Stewart (Methuen, 1978)
Gaia edited by Norman Myers (Doubleday, 1984) ✒
The Official World Wildlife Guide to Endangered Species of North America (Beacham Publishing, 1990). Two volumes
The Sinking Ark by Norman Myers (Pergamon, 1979)
State of the Ark by Lee Durrell (Doubleday, 1986) ✒
Vanishing Animals by Kurt Benirschke (Springer-Verlag, 1986) ✒
Where Have All the Wildflowers Gone? by Robert H. Mohlenbrock (Macmillan, 1983)

CHILDREN'S BOOKS

America's Endangered Birds (Morrow, 1979), **Gorilla** (Morrow, 1983), **Lili: A Giant Panda of Sichuan** (Morrow, 1988), **Rajpur: Last of the Bengal Tigers** (Morrow, 1979), and **Vanishing Wildlife of Latin America** (Morrow, 1981) are just a few of the books by Robert McClung about different endangered animals. Intermediate and Advanced
Animals in Danger is a series including the following titles: Asia, Europe, Forests of Africa, North America, and The Seas (The Rourke Corp., 1980). Intermediate and Advanced ✒
Animals in Danger: Trying to Save Our Wildlife (National Geographic Society, 1978). Primary ✒
The Auk, the Dodo, and the Oryx by Robert Silverberg (Crowell, 1967). Advanced
The Crocodile and the Crane by Judy Cutchins and Ginny Johnston (Morrow, 1986). Intermediate and Advanced
Endangered Animals is a series by J. M. Roever including the following titles: The Black-Footed Ferret, Brown Pelican, Mustangs, North American Eagles, Whooping Crane, and Wolves (Steck-Vaughn, 1972). Intermediate ✒
Endangered Plants by Dorothy Childs Hogner (Crowell, 1977). Intermediate
Endangered Predators by John Harris and Aleta Pahl (Doubleday, 1976). Advanced
Endangered Species by Christopher Lampton (Franklin Watts, 1988). Advanced
Endangered Species of the World is a series by Dr. Alvin Granowsky including the following titles with teachers' guides: Animals of the World, The Blue Whale, The Chinchilla, The Elephant, The Giraffe, The Giant Panda, The Gorilla, The Koala, The Rhinoceros, and The Tiger (Schoolhouse Press, 1986). Primary
Giant Condor of California by Julian May (Creative Educational Society, 1972). Primary
The Giant Panda by Jin Xugi and Markus Kappeler (G.P. Putnam's Sons, 1986). Intermediate ✒
The Lorax by Dr. Seuss (Random House, 1971). Primary and Intermediate

Our Endangered Earth is a series by David Cook including the following titles: Birds, Environment, Land Animals, and Ocean Life (Crown, 1983). Intermediate and Advanced
Plants in Danger by Edward R. Ricciuti (Harper & Row, 1979). Advanced
Project Panda Watch by Miriam Schlein (Atheneum, 1984). Advanced
Saving Our Animal Friends (National Geographic Society, 1986). Primary ✒
There Really Was a Dodo by Esther S. and Bernard L. Gordon (Walck, 1974). Primary and Intermediate
Tracking Wild Chimpanzees by Joyce Powzyk (Lothrop, 1988). Intermediate and Advanced
Twilight of the Animal Kingdom: The Endangered Species by Larry Harris (Ward Ritchie, 1972). Advanced
Vanishing Habitats by Noel Simon (Gloucester, 1987) Advanced ✒
Wildlife Alert! (National Geographic Society, 1980). Intermediate and Advanced ✒
Wildlife in Danger by Robert Burton (Silver Burdett, 1983). Advanced
Wildlife Making a Comeback (National Geographic Society, 1987) Intermediate ✒
The Whooping Crane: A Comeback Story by Dorothy Hinshaw (Clarion, 1988). Intermediate and Advanced
The World's Vanishing Birds by Cyril Littlewood (Arco, 1972). Advanced
ZooBooks is a series about many animals and includes an issue entitled Endangered Animals. An accompanying teaching unit with activity sheets and a role-playing game is also available. Write Wildlife Education Ltd., #930 W. Washington St., Suite 14, San Diego, CA 92103. Intermediate and Advanced ✒

FILMS, FILMSTRIPS, AND VIDEOS

Carolina Biological Supply Co. has slide sets entitled Rare and Endangered Animals, Extinction, Rare and Endangered Birds and Reptiles of the World, and Rare and Endangered Mammals of the World. Also available in filmstrips with cassettes are Endangered Species and The Cheetah: Portrait of an Endangered Species. For more information write Carolina Biological Supply Co., 2700 York Rd., Burlington, NC 27215.
Conserving America, Champions of Wildlife (Advanced) is a video with accompanying activity and resource guide. Video and/or guide available from the National Wildlife Federation, 1400 16th St., NW, Washington, DC 20036-2266.
Educational Images has slide sets entitled Endangered and Extinct Animals and Rare and Endangered Animals I & II, among others. For a catalog write Educational Images, Ltd., P.O. Box 3456, West Side, Elmira, NY 14905.
The Last Chance (Advanced) is a film on endangered species from the National Zoo. **The Northern Elephant Seal** (Primary and Intermediate) explains in simple terms how genetic similarity may cause species such as the elephant seal to be endangered despite their large numbers. Available from Bullfrog Films Inc., Oley, PA 19547.
Protecting Endangered Animals (All Ages) is available in film or video from Karol Media, 22 Riverview Dr., Wayne, NJ 07470-3191.
Pupfish of the Desert (All Ages) is a film from Stanton Films, 2417 Artesia Blvd., Redondo Beach, CA 90278.
Vanishing Animals of North America (Advanced) and **Vanishing from the Earth** (Advanced) are filmstrips with cassettes available from National Geographic Society, Educational Services, Dept. 90, Washington, DC 20036.

BOOKLETS, COLORING BOOKS, GAMES, AND POSTERS

Biologues is a series of fact sheets on endangered species from the U.S. Fish and Wildlife Service. They are free to teachers and club leaders. Write U.S. Fish and Wildlife Service, Attn: Publications Unit, Rm 130, 4401 N. Fairfax Dr., Arlington, VA 22203.

Carolina Biological Supply Co. has a board game called *Endangered Species* (Advanced), as well as endangered species rummy cards. For more information write Carolina Biological Supply Co., 2700 York Rd., Burlington, NC 27215.

Center for Marine Conservation has a coloring book called *Sea Turtles* and posters of sea turtles and other sea animals available to teachers at a discount. For more information write Center for Marine Conservation, 1725 DeSales St., NW, Suite 500, Washington, DC 20036.

Massachusetts Audubon Society has *Curious Naturalist* reprints entitled "New Citizens" (introduced species), "Lost Habitats," "Geography and Survival," "Special Needs for Survival," "The Alien Invasion" (introduced species), "Wildlife & Man's Chemicals," "Wildlife & Agriculture," "Over-Collecting Wildlife," and "The Ecology of Extinction." For an order form write Massachusetts Audubon Society, Educational Resource Office, Lincoln, MA 01773.

National Science Teacher's Association (NSTA) has two extinction posters. Write NSTA, 1742 Connecticut Ave., NW, Washington DC 20009.

OTHER ACTIVITY SOURCES

International Crane Foundation has seven different activity packets about cranes for various age levels. The packets contain background information, activity sheets, and puzzles. The ICF also has films and videos available for rent. For more information write International Crane Foundation, E-11376 Shady Lane Rd., Baraboo, WI 53913-9778.

Project WILD, developed by the Western Regional Environmental Education Council, Salina Star Route, Boulder, CO 80302, has endangered species-related activities including "Here Today, Gone Tomorrow," "Planting Animals," "Too Close for Comfort," and "Deadly Links."

The Nature Conservancy has educator packets and general information on endangered species. For more information write to The Nature Conservancy, 1815 N. Lynn St., Arlington, VA 22209.

Most **State Offices of Conservation** or **Fish and Wildlife** offer residents of their states lists of endangered species, curriculum packets, films, posters, pamphlets, coloring books, and other educational materials. Write to your state department of conservation and natural resources, or department of fish and wildlife, for information.

World Wildlife Fund has "Buyer Beware" brochures on illegal wildlife trade and a *Wildlife Trade Education Kit* containing background information, activities, and a slide program. For information write TRAFFIC(U.S.A.), World Wildlife Fund, 1250 24th St., NW, Washington, DC 20037.

Zero Population Growth, Inc., has activity kits on human population growth entitled *Elementary Population Activities Kit* and *EdVentures in Population Education Kit*. For information write Zero Population Growth, Inc., 1400 16th St., NW, Suite 320, Washington, DC 20036.

SOFTWARE

The Balance in Nature (Intermediate and Advanced). Using imaginary animals in a marine environment, along with colorful graphics and questions, this program introduces the concepts of food chains, adaptation, survival, and extinction. Available for Apple and Commodore 64. For a catalog of this and other programs write Focus Media, Inc., 839 Stewart Ave., P.O. Box 865, Garden City, NY 11530.

WHERE TO GET MORE INFORMATION

- aquariums and oceanariums
- botanical gardens
- college and university departments of botany, biology, conservation, or natural resources
- natural history museums
- nature centers
- zoos

Ranger Rick Endangered Species Index

Ranger Rick, *published by the National Wildlife Federation, is a monthly nature magazine for elementary-age children.*

WILDLIFE LAWS AND WHAT THEY MEAN

Endangered Species Act: (1973) This comprehensive law was passed to protect plants and animals that are in danger of becoming extinct. Species that are officially listed as *threatened* or *endangered* on the U.S. Fish and Wildlife Service list are not allowed to be imported or exported; hunted, collected, or harassed; transported across state or national lines for commerce; sold; or used in any way without an authorized permit from the U.S. Fish and Wildlife Service. Restrictions on trade and transport apply to live and dead animals and plants, their parts, and the products manufactured from them.

Protected species may be used only for the purposes of scientific research, public education, exhibition in zoos, or efforts that could help save the species. A few threatened species, such as American alligators, may be harvested in limited numbers in some areas.

Convention on International Trade in Endangered Species of Wild Fauna and Flora (CITES): (1975) This international treaty, which was designed to protect plants and animals affected by international trade, regulates the import and export of endangered and threatened wildlife. Nations that sign the treaty agree to restrict the trade of certain species. (Nearly 100 nations have signed.) These restrictions depend on the appendix each of the species is listed under.

- *Appendix I* includes species immediately threatened with extinction. All shipments of live and dead animals and plants, their parts, and any goods manufactured from them must have *two* permits—one from the exporting country and one from the importing country. These permits are granted only for educational or scientific purposes, and only if collection will not threaten the species.
- *Appendix II* includes species that are not immediately threatened by extinction, but will be if their trade is not regulated. A permit from only the exporting country is required. It's legal to use these species in commercial trade, but only if it will not threaten the species.
- *Appendix III* includes species that are not covered by Appendices I or II, but are endangered or threatened in a country that needs international help to protect them. An export permit must be issued by the country where it is in trouble.

Note: Nations belonging to CITES can take a "reservation" on certain species, which means they can exempt themselves from CITES requirements.

Lacey Act: (1900) This U.S. act prohibits the taking, selling, buying, importing, exporting , or transporting of any species (including rare plants and fish) that is protected by any state, federal, tribal, or foreign law.

The act also makes it illegal to import any species into the United States that may be harmful to people, agriculture, or wildlife. And it requires that wildlife be transported humanely and be correctly identified. Its strict penalties (up to $20,000 fine and/or five years' imprisonment) are often used to prosecute commercial traffickers.

Other Acts: Three other acts have been passed to protect specific groups of animals. The *Marine Mammal Protection Act* (1972) prohibits taking or harming marine mammals in U.S. waters, or importing their body parts and products. (Marine mammals include polar bears, sea otters, walruses, dugongs, manatees, whales, seals, and sea lions.) The *Migratory Bird Treaty Act* (1918) protects migratory birds and restricts trade of their body parts, feathers, nests, eggs, and products made from them. Seasonal hunting is allowed for some ducks, geese, woodcocks, and other migratory birds. A separate act, the *Eagle Protection Act* (1940), was passed to protect bald eagles and amended in 1962 to include golden eagles.

For a more complete list of the restrictions placed on endangered and threatened species, or for more information about these laws, write to the U.S. Fish and Wildlife Service, Office of Endangered Species, Washington, DC 20240.

1997 Update

Table Of Contents

THE PRAIRIE DOG CONNECTION

by Stephen C. Torbit, Ph.D.

July, 1976

ow! There goes another one!" I said to myself as another bolt of lightning flashed nearby. It was the Bicentennial—our nation's 200th birthday—and I was watching the best Fourth of July light show ever, all by myself.

I was a lone biologist searching for the elusive black-footed ferret on the Pawnee National Grasslands of northeastern Colorado. The Endangered Species Act (ESA) was three years old, and ferrets were one of the original species on the endangered species list.

The only known remaining population of ferrets, in South Dakota, had recently died out. We knew ferrets depend completely on prairie dogs for their food and shelter, but we didn't know much else about how ferrets relate to their environment or what their other needs are. I believe that during that search in 1976 I caught a glimpse of a black-footed ferret—possibly the last recorded observation in Colorado.

Sometime In 1990

"There just have to be more large prairie dog towns!" I exclaimed to my friends, Bob Oakleaf and Bob Luce of the Wyoming Game and Fish Department. One last colony of ferrets had been discovered at Meetetsee, Wyoming, and saved from extinction. Eighteen ferrets had been captured and placed in a captive breeding center in Sybille, Wyoming. Experts had learned how to breed ferrets in captivity. Now we had enough ferrets born every year to begin releasing them back into the wild.

Since 1976, we had learned a lot. We knew how many prairie dogs a single ferret needs to eat in a year and how many prairie dogs it takes to provide food for a mother ferret with *kits*—ferret babies. We knew how many prairie dogs have to be in a prairie dog colony for the colony to survive predation—hunting—by ferrets. We knew how much territory a ferret covers in its nightly hunting trips.

Now, in 1990, I was a ferret biologist working for the U.S. Fish and Wildlife Service, the government agency in charge of saving endangered species. I was working with the Wyoming Fish and Game Department to find a place to reintroduce ferrets in Wyoming and then in other Western states. But we had a big problem.

Where Are All The Prairie Dogs?

As we worked to save the ferret from extinction, we always assumed we'd be able to find plenty of prairie dog colonies of the right size where we could release ferrets back into their natural habitat. Now that we had found another ferret colony, we were sure we would be able to encourage the ferret population to grow and expand into other western states. Most important of all, we felt sure that we would be able to remove ferrets from the endangered species list.

Our problem was that it was turning out to be very, very hard to find prairie dog colonies—called *complexes*—big enough to support the ferrets we were eager to release. We had another, even bigger problem. The loss of large prairie dog colonies meant that other species might soon be in trouble, too.

What we were discovering was a signal that the prairie ecosystem itself had changed dramatically. Soon the whole ecosystem would probably show signs of change. The changes would make it hard for us to predict how long the prairie soil would stay fertile. The changes might lead to the loss of plants and animals adapted to life on the prairie the way it used to be. Populations of plants and animals might decrease, just as ferrets and prairie dogs had. The Endangered Species list

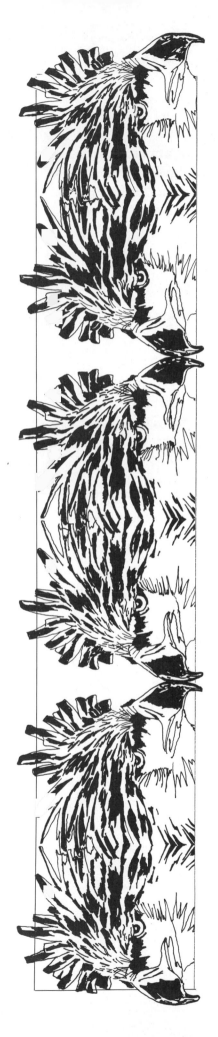

would get longer. As we realized what these signals meant, our hopes for getting the ferret off the list dimmed.

What Happened?

For more than 100 years, humans plowed, paved, and built on prairie dog colonies as we settled the West. We continue to pave over them today. We have also eliminated prairie dog towns by using poison. This has gone on for generations, because people believed that prairie dogs compete with cattle and sheep for the grasses and herbs that grow on the prairie. The result is that we have eliminated prairie dogs from over 90 percent of their historical territory. And now we know that prairie dogs probably don't compete with cattle and sheep for food as much as we used to believe.

Look Back In Time

Try to imagine what the great North American prairies looked like 200 years ago, before the plow and the bulldozer began to change them. The grass seems endless. Everywhere there are large grazing animals such as bison, elk, deer, and pronghorn antelope. There are many small rodents and, especially, a great many prairie dogs. If prairie dogs compete with large grazers, how is it that millions of bison and millions of pronghorn antelope can survive on the prairie with tens of millions of prairie dogs? The answer is that prairie dogs have never been a large threat to grazing animals.

As you continue to look back at the prairie of 200 years ago, you can see how prairie dogs help other animals survive. The burrow system of a prairie dog town provides shelter from the scorching sun, thunderstorms, winds, and winter snows for many small mammals and birds. Burrowing owls build their nests inside abandoned prairie dog burrows. Deer mice, cottontail rabbits, weasels, and black-footed ferrets use prairie dog burrows to raise their young. Amphibians and reptiles find shelter there, too.

Imagine you are watching a predator search for prey on the historical prairie. Hawks, eagles, badgers, and coyotes are drawn to the prairie dog colonies because all the other animals there are a rich source of food. Even if the predator can't catch a prairie dog, there might be a deer mouse, rabbit, or toad.

Because some kinds of prairie dogs remain active during winter, they provide food for birds of prey that migrate from the northern United States and Canada. Prairie dogs that are active above ground on sunny winter days are food for snowy owls and eagles.

What Now?

It was now clear that we had a very big problem. Without colonies large enough to support black-footed ferrets, how could the prairies continue to support the other species that have evolved to find food and shelter in prairie dog towns? As a result of the years of poisoning campaigns, most of the prairie dog colonies that still existed were too small to support ferrets, and therefore less valuable to other animals.

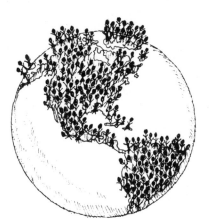

We finally did find areas in the Shirley Basin in Wyoming, the Badlands National Park in South Dakota, and along the Missouri River in Montana to reintroduce black-footed ferrets. They are beginning to breed and successfully raise their young. That means we have wild ferrets for the first time since 1987.

My friends and I still worry about finding enough large prairie dog towns. The recovery plan for ferrets calls for ten reintroduction sites across the West, but we have not been able to find ten good sites. We had figured out how to save the ferret, but now we faced a serious problem regarding prairie dogs. We must find a way to conserve the prairie dog. If we don't, the black-footed ferret may be doomed to live only in zoos and other areas of confinement.

That's the prairie dog connection. If we lose the prairie dog, we lose a lot. We may see a world in which eagles do not soar majestically over the prairie, where North America's only ferret does not stalk the night in search of prey, and where we can no longer hear the chirping of prairie dogs calling out across the prairie.

THE HABITAT CHALLENGE

by Richard Block

Students and teachers often use zoos and aquariums as a resource for studying endangered species. Whether you're on a class field trip or an outing with your family, these are good places to begin to understand more about our world's threatened resources. Many popular animals are found in zoos across the country: the African elephant, black rhinoceros, snow leopard, scarlet macaw, mandrill, jaguar, and zebra. For some rarer animals, such as the Siberian tiger, Addra gazelle, Guam kingfisher, golden lion tamarin, or black-footed ferret, there are more individuals in zoos than there are in the wild! When you visit a zoo or aquarium, you can observe and study these animals in exhibits that resemble their natural homes.

A Living Community

Whether you are working on a school assignment or visiting a zoo or aquarium with your friends or family, you may be tempted to focus on individual animals. But it is important to remember that each plant and animal is part of a living community. Their home, or habitat, is filled with other plants and animals, and each one has an important role in making life possible for other species. Just as *NatureScope: Endangered Species* points out in "The Habitat Connection," protecting habitat is the most important issue in saving plants and animals. We all need a place to live!

Today, zoos and aquariums are learning how to protect and care for animals outside their natural homes—in special exhibits designed to look something like their homes in the wild. In some cases, zoos and aquariums have been able to return animals to their wild homes. Some of these animals are described in the chapter "Bouncing Back." From golden lion tamarins to bald eagles, animals have been returned successfully to the wild.

But they all had one thing in common: they all had a place to go—they all had habitat.

Protecting Populations By Protecting Habitat

Many zoos that have hatched bald eagle chicks have been able to help rebuild wild populations of eagles. The Cincinnati Zoo has provided the Ohio Department of Natural Resources with chicks that were then placed into the nests of adult eagles. The adult eagles, which had no chicks of their own, raised these "adopted" offspring and taught them how to survive in the wild. But having more eagle chicks was only part of the solution to saving bald eagles. Just as "Poachers, Poisons, & Other Problems" (page 34) describes, the eagles' chances of survival were increased when the chemical pesticide DDT was no longer used on crops. Reduction of these chemicals in the eagles' habitat allowed young birds to grow up healthy and raise chicks of their own.

golden lion tamarin

The Space Question

How much habitat does an animal or plant need? Don't let the size of a zoo or aquarium exhibit fool you! Caring for the animals in a zoo or aquarium takes much more space and many more resources than you can see in the exhibit. The animals' food is brought to the exhibit every day. Water is purified, filtered, and pumped or carried to the exhibit from outside sources. The animals are protected by buildings or structures created to resemble the dens, cavities, or dense vegetation naturally used by the animals.

In the wild, plants and animals may require very large spaces to meet their needs for survival. "Sizing Up Reserves" (pages 32–33) provides a good introduction to the importance of space. For example, an individual jaguar requires more than 17,000 acres of habitat in order to survive—just over 26 square miles. That's the area needed to provide enough prey species to eat and enough places to find adequate cover for just one jaguar! The space required for an entire population of jaguars to survive would be much larger—as much as 13,000 square miles, an area about 11 times the size of the state of Rhode Island.

Of course, there are some species that have much more restricted ranges. The Devil's Hole pupfish is found only in one small pool on the Ash Meadows National Wildlife Refuge in Nevada. Most of the pupfish's life takes place in 128 square feet—a space that would fit inside most classrooms several times. But even in this case, the area required to protect the pupfish's survival is much larger than its immediate habitat. The water level in the pool is affected by the level of water under the ground—the water table. When water is pumped out of the ground for use by people, even some distance from the wildlife refuge, the water level in the pool can drop so low that the pupfish might not survive.

Long-Range Planning

Then there's another challenge. What about species that migrate or move great distances? Protecting their habitat may take a lot of planning. The whooping cranes fly 2,500 miles each spring to reach their nesting grounds in Wood Buffalo National Park in Northwest Territories, Canada. Each fall, these same birds, accompanied by the young cranes, fly 2,500 miles back to their winter feeding grounds on Aransas National Wildlife Refuge on the Gulf coast of Texas. That's 5,000 miles a year—like driving from New York City to Las Vegas and back again! For the whooping cranes, it's not only important to protect the habitats where they nest in the summer and feed in the winter; it's important to protect the places where they stop to rest and eat on their long trip between destinations.

Pieces In A Puzzle

Habitat is the key. All animals need places and space in which to grow and reproduce. Without the right habitat, their chances of survival are not good. It's reassuring to know that the animals in zoos and aquariums represent populations of animals that survive in the wild. It's sad to think that some of these animals could no longer be found in the wild places they once roamed. From deserts to tropical rain forests, the world is filled with species adapted to survive in different habitats. Like the pieces of a puzzle, each plant and animal fits together to play its own special role. And each one depends on its shared habitat for survival.

Action!

Understanding more about our world and the priceless wildlife and plant treasures that live here is a good start. But it will take more than understanding to make a difference. It will take action! Zoos and aquariums must continue to do what they can for endangered species in need of immediate help. It's up to everyone to find ways to protect habitat—from our own backyards to distant habitats on the other side of the world. "People power" is just the first step in the lifelong adventure of understanding and caring for our world's wildlife treasures.

Talk About It!

ivory-billed woodpecker

- What migratory species of animals are found where you live? Where do they travel, and what do they need to survive? Use a map to aid in the discussion. A few examples of migratory species include songbirds, shorebirds, bats, whales, and insects such as the monarch butterfly. What species in your zoo or aquarium are migratory?

- Discuss what role a zoo or aquarium plays in your community. Is it involved with conservation or education? Does it offer special classes or programs to help people learn about wildlife?

- How can you use a zoo or aquarium to help you learn more about wildlife? Discuss activities that you might create to use a zoo or aquarium as a laboratory. Can you think of games or contests involving the plants and animals in the zoo or aquarium?

- Imagine that you're the director of your zoo or aquarium. Discuss any changes you might make. What new animals would you add? What exhibits would you change? What activities would you create to help people learn more about wildlife?

- Let's look into the future! What do you think will happen to wildlife habitat where you live, elsewhere in this country, and around the world? What role do you think zoos and aquariums can play in the future to help animal species survive?

DECISION TIME IN SURINAME

by Thane Maynard

inding ways to protect wild animals and plants is complicated, especially when they are in danger of extinction. It takes cooperation among government officials, scientists, conservationists, business people, and ordinary people, who all must be willing to make tough choices. One way to see what it takes is to look at a case study—an example from the real world. At the Cincinnati Zoo, where I work, some of our real-world conservation efforts are taking place far away in the rain forests of South America.

Over the past four years, the Cincinnati Zoo's Conservation Fund has supported many different wildlife projects in the country of Suriname, on the northern coast of South America. Conservation International, the wildlife organization most involved in protecting tropical forests, is our partner.

Reaching Different Audiences

We are producing three videos that encourage people to help protect Suriname's rain forests. We need three different tapes because each one aims at a different audience. The main tape is for members of the Surinamese Parliament and other government decision makers. It encourages them to think about how to plan for the best long-term use of their forests and develop ways to protect the country, its people, and forests. The second tape will be shown on Suriname's national television network. It celebrates the importance of Suriname's amazing *biodiversity*—the rich variety of plant and animal life found there.

The third video is being produced for Americans. We hope to show people in our country the wonders of Suriname and encourage them to travel there as tourists to see it for themselves. This kind of traveling is called *ecotourism* because tourists go there primarily to experience the natural environment.

What's Special About Suriname?

Suriname is on the northern coast of South America, surrounded by Guyana, Brazil, and French Guyana. It's about the size of the state of Georgia in the United States. But this very small country is home to a very large number of plants, animals, and insects. There are 184 species of mammals, 670 species of birds, 152 species of reptiles, 95 species of amphibians, and more than 300 kinds of fish! And that's not even counting the *invertebrates*—animals without backbones. There are thousands of species of insects, and some of them haven't even been described yet by *entomologists*—scientists who study insects. Suriname has plenty of plants, too—more than 5,300 different species.

One reason for Suriname's rich biodiversity is that so much of the country is covered by forest—85 percent of the land. The vast majority of Suriname's people live on the remaining 15 percent of the land. Only 5 percent of the people live in the "interior"—the vast, undeveloped tropical forest that covers so much of the country. Rain forests offer the most diverse habitats in the world—and this huge forest is inhabited by very few people. This means that wildlife can flourish without human interference.

Still, many of Suriname's plants and animals are endangered. Habitat destruction and overuse by people are part of the problem. But another cause is that so many of the plant and animal species in Suriname are *endemic*—found only in a single area in the world. If they are not preserved in Suriname, they will be lost to us. Two kinds of bats, one kind of reptile, and six kinds of amphibians in Suriname are endemic. There are also more than 200 endemic plants. Finding such a large number of endemic species in such a small country is remarkable. By comparison, the state of Ohio, where I live, is about the same size as Suriname—and we have no endemic species at all.

"Save The Blue Frog"

One of Suriname's endemic species is also one of the most beautiful creatures on earth—the blue poison dart frog. As a defense against predators, poison dart frogs produce a strong poisonous mucus that covers their bodies. Their bright blue color gives a warning: This frog is poison! The poison dart frog's name comes from a tradition of South American tribes. These hunters coat the tips of hunting darts with the poisonous mucus to stun or kill their prey.

We chose the poison dart frog, which lives only in southern Suriname, as the symbol for our public education campaign. Now posters, T-shirts, and booklets for kids in villages and schools throughout Suriname send out the message loud and clear: *"Kibri den okopipi!"* It means, "Save the blue frog!" The idea isn't just to promote a really cool amphibian. The blue dart frog is also a source of national pride. That's why the other theme of the program is *"Sranan—Sabi San Yu Abi"* or "Suriname—Know What You Have!"

Because of their restricted range, endemic species such as the poison dart frog are unusually rare to begin with. When there is even the smallest amount of pressure from human activities, many quickly become endangered.

People Are The Key

There are eight national parks in Suriname. They offer some of the most beautiful and biologically important areas in the nation. But like our parks in the United States, these areas are relatively small, protecting less than 4 percent of Suriname's forests. The people who live in the forests surrounding these national parks are the key in protecting wilderness areas. The forest provides these tribes with the food and shelter they need for survival. In return, the tribes provide protection from intruders whose activities could threaten the forest's plant and animal life.

This is the best hope for protecting Suriname's forests—relying on the way the country's traditional tribal lands are protected now. Saving rain forests in South America isn't just about protecting poison dart frogs, jaguars, parrots, and boa constrictors. It's about people, too—people who have lived in and depended on the forest for thousands of years.

But protecting Suriname's rain forests is even more complicated than that.

Difficult Choices

In Suriname, timber has been a major *export*, or material leaving the country, for more than one hundred years. The logging has been done by carefully selecting and taking out only the trees most valuable for lumber instead of *clearcutting*—cutting down all the trees in an area. This kind of timber production preserves the forest habitat and also provides jobs for Surinamese workers.

But today, the leaders and people of Suriname face some difficult choices. Huge logging companies from Korea, Indonesia, and Malaysia want to purchase the right to clearcut millions of acres of trees and grind up the wood to make paper. Their factory ships are already offshore, waiting for contracts to be signed.

Economic problems in Suriname are forcing policy makers to make hard decisions about the future of their country. Can they afford to protect the vast interior where so few people live? Can they afford to say "no" to the money from huge logging companies waiting offshore?

Fortunately, there are better choices. One is carefully managed logging that preserves the forest habitat for people, plants, and animals. Another is a strong ecotourism program that brings more travelers from other countries to visit Suriname's remarkable rain forests. Tourist dollars will then help support the country.

It will take the work of many different kinds of people to protect the endangered species in Suriname. Researchers, scientists, politicians, teachers, business leaders, and village elders are all working to create a bright future for their people, their country, *and* their wildlife. If they succeed in saving the rain forest and the poison dart frog, these things will pay them back by becoming travel attractions and will support Suriname for generations to come.

EXISTING & PROPOSED PROTECTED AREAS IN SURINAME

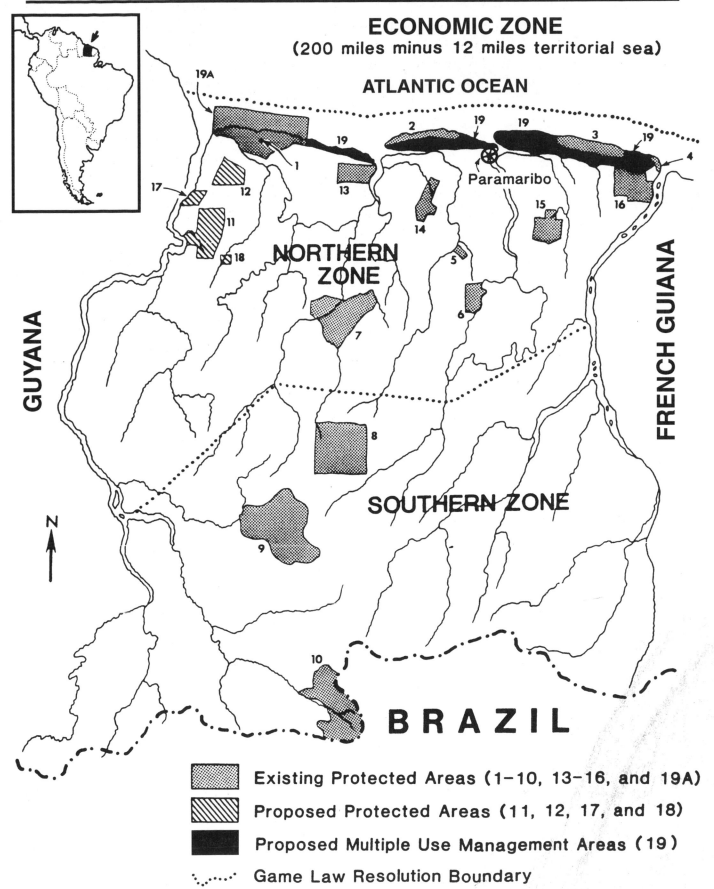

ECONOMIC ZONE
(200 miles minus 12 miles territorial sea)

ATLANTIC OCEAN

Paramaribo

GUYANA

FRENCH GUIANA

NORTHERN ZONE

SOUTHERN ZONE

BRAZIL

N

Existing Protected Areas (1–10, 13–16, and 19A)

Proposed Protected Areas (11, 12, 17, and 18)

Proposed Multiple Use Management Areas (19)

Game Law Resolution Boundary

Bibliography Update

Note: A * at the end of a listing indicates that the book is a good source of endangered species pictures.

GENERAL REFERENCE BOOKS

Birds in Jeopardy by Paul Ehrlich, David Dobkin, and Darryl Wheye (Stanford University Press, 1992)

The Diversity of Life by Edward O. Wilson (Belknap/Harvard University Press, 1992)

Gaia: An Atlas of Planet Management edited by Norman Myers (Doubleday, 1993) *

International Wildlife Trade: Whose Business Is It? by Sarah Fitzgerald (World Wildlife Fund, 1989)

The Official World Wildlife Fund Guide to Endangered Species of North America in three volumes (Beacham, 1990, 1992)

Vanishing Flora: Endangered Plants Around the World by Dugald Stermer (Abrams, 1995) *

Where Have All the Birds Gone? by John Terborgh (Princeton University Press, 1989)

CHILDREN'S BOOKS

Aardvarks, Disembark! by Ann Jonas (Puffin, 1994). Primary

And Then There Was One: The Mysteries of Extinction by Margery Facklam (Little Brown, 1993). Intermediate

Animals In Danger by Melvin Berger (Ranger Rick Science Spectacular Series, Newbridge Comms., 1993). Primary to Intermediate

At Home in the Rainforest by Diane Willow (Charlesbridge, 1992). Primary

The Call of the Wolves by Jim Murphy (Scholastic, 1989). Intermediate *

The Crocodile and the Crane by Judy Cutchins and Ginny Johnston (Morrow, 1986). Intermediate and Advanced

Endangered Animals by Dean Morris (Raintree, 1990). Primary

Endangered Animals is part of the Zoobook series and includes teaching unit, activity sheets, and games (Wildlife Education Ltd., 930 W. Washington St., Suite 14, San Diego, CA 92103). Intermediate and Advanced *

Endangered Species by Sunni Bloyd (Lucent Books, 1989). Advanced

Extinction by Rebecca Stefoff (Chelsea, 1992). Advanced

Extremely Weird Endangered Species by Sarah Lovett (John Muir, 1992). Intermediate *

Lili: A Giant Panda of Sichuan by Robert McClung (Morrow, 1988). Intermediate

Living Treasure: Saving Earth's Threatened Biodiversity by Laurence Pringle (Morrow, 1991). Intermediate and Advanced

The Orangutan by Ruth Ashby (Dillon, 1994). Advanced *

Pandas by Jinny Johnson (Highlights, 1991). Intermediate *

Tracking Wild Chimpanzees by Joyce Powzyk (Lathrop, 1988). Primary

Tropical Rain Forests is part of the Our Endangered Planet series by Cornelia Mutel (Lerner, 1993). Intermediate and Advanced

Usborne Green Guides: Protecting Endangered Species by Felicity Brooks (EDC, 1991). Intermediate

V for Vanishing: An Alphabet of Endangered Animals by Patricia Mullins (Harper Collins, 1993). Primary

The Whooping Crane: A Comeback Story by Dorothy Hinshaw Patent (Clarion, 1993). Advanced

Will We Miss Them? Endangered Species by Alexandra Wright (Charlesbridge, 1992). Primary to Intermediate *

hawksbill sea turtle

Videos, Films, And Slides

Conserving America, Champions of Wildlife (Advanced) is a video. For more information write to:
V.I.E.W. Video
34 E. 23rd St.
NY, NY 10010
U.S.A.

Endangered and Extinct Animals and **Rare and Endangered Animals*** are slide sets with guides. For more information write to:
Educational Images Ltd.
Box 3456 W
Elmira, NY 14905
U.S.A.

Endangered Species (Advanced) is a set of four videos or filmstrips with skill booster sheets on "Understanding the Problem," "Endangered Land Animals," "Endangered Water Animals," and "Endangered Animals of the Air." For more information write to:
SVE
6677 N. Northwest Hwy.
Chicago, IL 60631
U.S.A.

The Last Chance (Advanced) and **The Northern Elephant Seal** (Primary and Intermediate) are films. For more information write to:
Bullfrog Films
Box 149
Oley, PA 19547
U.S.A.

Protecting Endangered Animals (Intermediate and Advanced) is a video. For a catalog write to:
National Geographic Society
Educational Services
P.O. Box 98019
Washington, DC 20090-8019
U.S.A.

Rare and Endangered Animals, **Rare and Endangered Birds and Reptiles of the World**, and **Rare and Endangered Mammals of the World** are slide sets. For more information write to:
Carolina Biological Supply
2700 York Rd.
Burlington, NC 27215
U.S.A.

Saving Endangered Animals (Intermediate and Advanced) comes in video or videodisc format from Scientific American Frontiers and includes the program "Rescuing the Great Bustard," teacher's guide, and activity sheets. For more information write to:
SVE
6677 N. Northwest Hwy.
Chicago, IL 60631
U.S.A.

Sea Turtles and **Whales** (Advanced) are slide shows with scripts. For more information write to:
Center for Marine Conservation
1725 DeSales St., NW
Washington, DC 20036
U.S.A.

Vulnerable, Threatened, Endangered, Extinct (Intermediate) is a video. For more information write to:
AIMS Multimedia
9710 DeSoto Ave.
Chatsworth, CA 91311-4409
U.S.A.

dodo

BROCHURES, COLORING BOOKS, GAMES, POSTERS, AND FACT SHEETS

Biologues is a series of fact sheets on endangered species and the official U.S. list of endangered species. They are free to teachers and club leaders. For more information write to:
U.S. Fish & Wildlife Service
Attn: Publications Unit
18th & C Streets, NW
Washington, DC 20240
U.S.A.

For other brochures and materials, write:
Chief, Division of Endangered Species
U.S. Fish & Wildlife Service
4401 N. Fairfax Dr., Rm. 452
Arlington, VA 22203
U.S.A.

Defenders of Wildlife offers free sets of 25 fact sheets, posters with a different animal on each side, species lists, and brochures. Write to:
Defenders of Wildlife
1101 14th St. NW, Suite 1400
Washington, DC 20005
U.S.A.

Endangered Animals Dot-to-Dot, by Monica Russo, includes background information on 39 species worldwide and activity sheets to connect-the-dots and color. (Sterling, 1994).

Endangered Species (Advanced) is available as a board game and as endangered species rummy cards. For more information write to:
Carolina Biological Supply Co.
2700 York Rd.
Burlington, NC 27215
U.S.A.

Manatee Coloring Book contains posters of sea turtles and fact sheets on whales and other sea animals. For more information write to:
Center for Marine Conservation
1725 DeSales St. NW
Washington, DC 20036
U.S.A.

National Science Teacher's Association has two posters on extinction. Write to:
NSTA
1840 Wilson Blvd.
Arlington, VA 22201-3000
U.S.A.

OTHER ACTIVITY SOURCES

Endangered Species of the World (Primary) is a set of readers, teacher's guide, and skillmasters (Modern Curriculum, 1989). For more information write to:
Modern Curriculum
299 Jefferson Rd.
Parsippany, NJ 07054–0480

International Crane Foundation has three different activity packets about cranes, as well as posters, photos, and books. The ICF also has films, videos, and slide shows available for rent. For more information write to:
ICF
E-11376 Shady Lane Rd.
P.O. Box 447
Baraboo, WI 53913-0447
U.S.A.

Project WILD has endangered species-related activities, including "Here Today, Gone Tomorrow," "Too Close for Comfort," and others. For more information write to:
Western Regional Environmental Education Council
5430 Grosvenor Ln.
Bethesda, MD 20814
U.S.A.

Whales: Activities Based on Research from the Center for Coastal Studies (Primary) is a book that includes student activities and background information on whale behavior, communication, and research (Scholastic, 1992; available from Penguin USA, P.O. Box 120, Bergenfield, NJ 07621).

World Wildlife Fund has "Buyer Beware" brochures on illegal wildlife trade and a *Wildlife Trade Education Kit* containing background information, species fact sheets, activities, and a slide program. For more information write to:
TRAFFIC (U.S.A.)
World Wildlife Fund
1250 24th St. NW
Washington, DC 20037
U.S.A.

brown hyena

SOFTWARE

Discovering Endangered Wildlife (Intermediate and Advanced) This CD-ROM teaches about 50 species' habitat, habits, and threats to survival with games, puzzles, photographs, video clips, sounds, narration, and printable fact sheets. Available for Windows. Write to:
CLEARVUE/eav
6465 N. Avondale Ave.
Chicago, IL 60631-1996
U.S.A.

Encyclopedia of U.S. Endangered Species (Intermediate and Advanced) is a CD-ROM with detailed information about 700 protected plants and animals, including location, habitat, biology, and survival threats. The program features multimedia presentations, color photos, and sounds, and includes interactive questions, quizzes, and glossary. Write to:
Zane Publishing
1950 Stemmons, Suite 4044
Dallas, TX 75207-3109
U.S.A.

WHERE TO GET MORE INFORMATION

- state departments of conservation, natural resources, or fish and wildlife—most offer to state residents educational materials on state-endangered species: lists, curriculum packets, films, posters, pamphlets, coloring books, or others
- aquaria and oceanaria
- botanical gardens
- college and university departments of botany, biology, conservation, or natural resources
- natural history museums
- nature centers
- zoos
- World Wide Web site: U.S. Fish and Wildlife Service can be reached at http://www/fws.gov

Internet Address Disclaimer
The Internet information provided here was correct, to the best of our knowledge, at the time of publication. It is important to remember, however, the dynamic nature of the Internet. Resources that are free and publicly available one day may require a fee or restrict access the next, and the location of items may change as menus and homepages are reorganized.